1979
Winners
of the American Society
of Newspaper Editors
Competition

BEST
NEWSPAPER
WRITING

Edited by
Roy Peter Clark

odern Media Institute
556 Central Avenue
St. Petersburg, Florida 33701

ISBN 0-935742-01-8
ISSN 0195-895X

Printed in the United States of America

ACKNOWLEDGMENTS

Grateful acknowledgment is made to the following for permission to reprint the newspaper articles included in this book:

The *Philadelphia Inquirer* and Richard Ben Cramer for the dispatches from the Middle East.

The *Boston Sunday Globe* and Tom Oliphant for selections from *The Globe's* special "Blizzard of '78" section.

The *New Bedford Standard-Times* and Everett S. Allen for the essays which appeared in the *Standard-Times*.

The *Fort Wayne News-Sentinel* and Mary Ellen Corbett for the feature series on Hal Corbett. Copyright © 1978 by Mary Ellen Corbett.

Modern Media Institute also would like to acknowledge a special debt to Marlene Shebu, without whose skills and dedication as production coordinator this book could not have been published.

PREFACE

"How good can newspaper writing be?" That question was put to me recently by George Edmonson, a young feature writer for the *Richmond News Leader*. At the time, we were discussing a 50-year-old essay by Henry J. Smith, the great managing editor of the *Chicago Daily News*. Four decades before Tom Wolfe discovered that journalistic writing could read like fiction, Smith was celebrating those great newspaper writers who "consider it proper, nay, necessary, to picture the strange jumble of human events in strokes as vivid, as touching, as humorous as the brush-marks of a novelist."

The era described by Smith passed years ago. In our time, editors and readers have come to realize that their papers are, for the most part, badly written. Distracted by the new newspaper technology, editors have abdicated their responsibility to train and encourage good writers. Journalism schools are graduating students ignorant of Standard English Usage.

In 1977 I undertook a project, with the blessings of the American Society of Newspaper Editors (ASNE), to improve the writing at the *St. Petersburg Times*. Since then newspaper editors have hired writing instructors, developed critical newsletters, organized seminars and posted memos to improve the skills of writers and editors. In less than two years, I have attended more than 30 newspaper conferences concerned with good writing.

The spirit of many of these meetings has been one of revival. But the revival has been based on a frustrated recognition of our collective sins. Newspapers are losing readers, and some editors are ready to try anything.

The same negative impulse has forced schools to introduce aspiring journalists to courses in grammar. When a university journalism professor sees the headline PSYCOLOGY RATED FAVORABLE in the school paper, he is likely to forget about training good writers and settle for a youngster who at least knows syntax from shinola.

This book has a different message. It says "Look how good we can be." It answers George Edmonson's question. It proves that newspaper writing can be very good, indeed. The work of four prize-winning journalists, presented in this volume, should convince editors, writers, journalism students and teachers — anyone who cares about the language — that there is hope. You can be a writer and still work for a newspaper.

Why are these stories so good? They are written by gifted storytellers who are also careful, thorough reporters. The writers share a sense of style and structure. And they all write about people.

This book should help dispel persistent myths about newspaper writing in America: that there is no room in newspapers for good writing; that reporting and writing are mutually exclusive skills; that deadlines make good writing impossible; that governmental or international news is, by definition, unreadable; that good writing can only be found in powerful papers with enormous resources.

These stories prove that if articles are well-written, newspapers will find room for them. They show that good reporting adds the detailed description, the anecdotes, the quotations that bring stories to life. Most of these stories were written quickly, some in "the white heat of frustration," as one writer puts it. By focusing on people rather then institutions, these writers bring home the dramatic consequences of governmental policy. And in response to the final myth, the one about good writing being only in the big papers, we are happy to introduce Everett S. Allen, who has been writing splendid prose in the *New Bedford (Mass.) Standard-Times* for 41 years.

The writers in this collection are very different. They range in age from 28 to 63. They include a freelancer, a foreign correspondent, a bureau reporter and an editorial writer.

The stories are different, too, ranging from Allen's timeless meditation on nature to Richard Ben Cramer's tale of a Jewish girl killed by Palestinian commandos. These rich stories speak for themselves. The notes and discussion sections are designed to stimulate interest in the writer's craft. That is why we tracked down these four talented writers and had them talk about their own work. In some cases, the stories about *how* these pieces were written are as fascinating as the written works themselves.

Newspaper writers learn early of the agony and the sweat that Faulkner described as every writer's lot. Having talked to each writer, I know there was agony and sweat invested in each carefully constructed sentence. The result is writing filled with fire and wisdom, stories that fulfill Faulkner's requirement for greatness: They look into the human heart.

Roy Peter Clark
November 6, 1979

CONTENTS

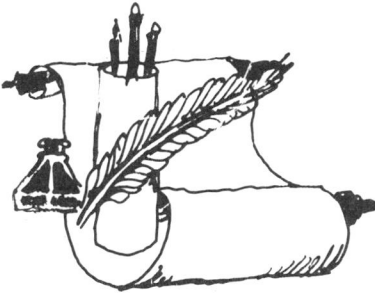

INTRODUCTION

On April 25, 1922 a small group of newspaper editors gathered in New York City to adopt the constitution of a new national organization dedicated to "the consideration of their common problems and the promotion of their professional ideals."

Today that association — The American Society of Newspaper Editors (ASNE) — has a membership of 870 and is recognized as the most prestigious organization of men and women who control the news and editorial content of America's daily newspapers.

The 75 editors gathered in New York 57 years ago agreed in the preamble of their constitution that a principal purpose of the ASNE would be to "work collectively for the solution of common problems." And in 1977-78, under the presidency of Eugene Patterson of *The St. Petersburg Times,* the Society identified as a major common problem the desperate need to improve the quality of writing in American newspapers.

Roy Peter Clark, Ph.D., an Auburn University professor and *St. Petersburg Times* writing coach, spent much of the year studying newspaper writing, and a major segment of the Society's 1978 convention was set aside for Clark's critical analysis and suggestions for making newspapers more readable.

The Society responded by backing Patterson's proposal for a contest to select and recognize the finest writing in American and Canadian newspapers each year starting in 1978. This book brings together the four winners announced at the ASNE's 1979 convention, accompanied by Clark's "Notes and Comments" and an interview with each of the winning writers. The winners, in four categories, were chosen from among more than 400 entries by this panel of 11 editors making up the ASNE Writing Awards Committee:

Thomas Winship, *Boston Globe*, Chairman

James K. Batten, *Knight-Ridder Newspapers*

Judith W. Brown, *New Britain (Conn.) Herald*

Edward R. Cony, *Wall Street Journal*

John O. Emmerich, Jr., *Greenwood (Miss.) Commonwealth*

Katherine Fanning, *Anchorage Daily News*

Philip Geyelin, *Washington Post*

James Hoge, *Chicago Sun-Times*

Maxwell McCrohon, *Chicago Tribune*

Claude Sitton, Raleigh (N.C.) *News and Observer*

William F. Thomas, *Los Angeles Times*

Modern Media Institute (MMI), the publisher of this volume, was founded four years ago by the late Nelson Poynter, board chairman of *The St. Petersburg Times* and *Congressional Quarterly*. Poynter gave stock in *The Times* to MMI, which spends its dividends developing and teaching unusual programs for media students and professionals.

This book, combining current examples of truly fine writing from daily newspapers and Roy Peter Clark's "Notes and Comments," should prove an invaluable aid to students and teachers of the craft.

The book is an "instant project" for Clark, who joined the MMI staff in September, 1979 after spending a year as a *Times* theater critic. As the book was going to press Clark was busily creating within the Institute a writing center which will sponsor a series of seminars for editors, writers and teachers throughout the year.

In addition to its emphasis on writing, MMI offers many opportunities for professionals and for students, from high school through graduate school. Here's a sampler:

• A dozen graduate students from around the country spend 12 weeks in St. Petersburg studying newspaper management.

- Fifteen young middle management professionals cover much the same ground in two to three weeks.
- Liberal arts majors with a yen to write for newspapers or magazines come to MMI twice a year for concentrated "how-to" courses.
- Each summer several dozen college and university students spend eight weeks at MMI polishing skills in writing, editing and illustration.
- High school students from the St. Petersburg area produce student newspapers in a modern type lab.
- Almost every weekend a group of students or teachers gather at MMI for concentrated workshops on a wide range of topics.

MMI's goals and the goals of ASNE in sponsoring competition to identify fine newspaper writing are so closely meshed that some would say this volume was inevitable.

Donald K. Baldwin
Director
Modern Media Institute

BEST
NEWSPAPER
WRITING

EDITOR'S NOTE: *EDITOR'S NOTE: Richard Ben Cramer, 28, is a native of Rochester, N.Y., and has degrees from Johns Hopkins and Columbia Universities. He worked as a reporter with the Baltimore Sun from 1972 to 1976. He joined the Philadelphia Inquirer, as transportation writer, in 1976. He was sent to Cairo for the Christmas Day 1977 negotiations between Anwar Sadat and Menachim Begin and remained as Middle East correspondent. His stories out of the Middle East were so poignant and powerful that they swept most of the important awards for international reporting, including the Pulitzer Prize. He is now stationed in London from where he covers Europe, Africa and the Middle East.*

The Philadelphia Inquirer, a member of the Knight-Ridder group, has a daily circulation of almost 420,000 and a Sunday circulation of more than 830,000.

1979

Prize Winner

News/Deadline

Richard Ben Cramer

MARCH 15, 1978

HAIFA, Israel — The Hadani family was sitting shiva. The house was filled with family and friends observing the ancient Jewish custom, a custom that surrounds the bereaved with the living so they will not dwell morbidly on the dead.

In the 48 hours since their daughter, Na'ami, who was 9, died in the Palestinian commando raid on the highway between here and Tel Aviv, Joseph and Levana Hadani have not been alone.

It was the same in a score of homes where the victims of the terrorists lived — neighbors and friends and family from all over Israel arriving to succor the survivors.

And it was the same, in a larger sense, throughout this tight little country, where everyone is touched by a single death and the

1

death of 36 Jews is a tragedy both national and personal.

In English, the rite acted out by the Hadanis is called "sitting shiva for the dead." But shiva is really for the living. The women bringing food and the men bringing news, and the coffee and the self-consciously normal talk are all designed to keep the family thinking in the present and looking to the future.

There is strength in feeling so much life around, warmth in kissing and being kissed.

In the Hadani home, the treatment was working. Joseph and Levana Hadani, their brothers and sisters and fathers, had gathered in a small room at one end of the apartment for part of the night to quietly tell their story.

When the story was told, Joseph Hadani left the room for a moment, walking stiffly because of his wounds. When he came back, he was followed by four of his co-workers, who gathered behind him in the doorway.

Hadani drew to him Ayelet, 10, the daughter who remains, and he said in English he had obviously rehearsed:

"We are not broken."

☐

It was to have been a festive occasion. Joseph Hadani's family and families of others in the national bus cooperative were on a sightseeing tour. Joseph, for a change, did not have to drive a bus.

His wife began her story.

"I heard a shot and I didn't know what happened. All the people in the bus were singing, and with accordion. Everyone was so happy. It was the end of the outing for the Egged (bus cooperative) and we were going back to Haifa.

"I heard the shots and I heard someone fall down, and I heard crying. I recognized my husband's voice and I began to cry, 'Yosi, Yosi, my husband'. I ran to the front and shouted to them to open the door of the bus."

Levana Hadani was one of the lucky ones. She and Ayelet had been sitting in the back of the bus, away from the first bursts of machine-gun fire that came from the roadside.

The first bullets flying through the windshield wounded her younger daughter, Na'ami, who had been sitting in the little jump seat beside the driver, and her husband, Joseph, who had been standing just behind.

When the bus stopped, some of the other Egged drivers pulled Joseph onto the asphalt. Mrs. Hadani lifted her wounded daughter and ran toward the traffic to flag down a car.

"The man who stopped put his own children out of the car to take me and my daughter. Then he saw in his mirror the terrorists coming back toward the bus and his own children were around the bus with the shooting.

"He said he could not take me and he put me out on the road again. Then he went back to get his children."

The man was too late. He died trying to rescue his children from the machine-gun fire.

"So, I waited on the road and stopped a man and a woman who just saw the bus stopped on the side of the road, that's all. They didn't recognize what was going on. They started to pass it and they saw a man pointing a gun at the bus. They said they thought it was a soldier gone mad."

She got Na'ami into their car.

"The man (got out) and went to the other side of the road and began to stop the cars coming from Haifa. I was in the back of the car. And the woman turned it and put it across the road to stop the other cars.

"I felt so helpless. I saw my daughter's eyes close. Her head was open, here, at the top — so much blood. And I see here in her jaw a big hole. She doesn't move, but she breathes.

"I left my other daughter in the bus. I forgot everything. I cried in the back of the car, 'She's dying, dying . . . quickly, please . . . the hospital.'"

In the car, Mrs. Hadani found a piece of cotton, a little piece which she held ineffectually against the large wound in her daughter's head. With her other hand, she picked broken teeth and chewing gum from Na'ami's open mouth.

Crying, leaning over her daughter and dabbing at the large wound, Mrs. Hadani said softly over and over, "Reh yhi ye beseder —It'll be all right."

"I thought maybe she can hear me, maybe I can give her courage," Mrs. Hadani said.

At the hospital, they quickly took Na'ami away. The doctors gently told Mrs. Hadani they would do what they could, but she had seen the wound in the head and she knew. Ten minutes later, her husband was wheeled in.

"He spoke and I heard him: 'Where is my daughter? What condition is she in? Is she alive?'

"I took his hand. I wanted him to know that I am with him. I told him, 'Don't worry, she breathes.'

"They take him and a doctor comes. I hear him speak with a nurse, with instructions about my husband — 'Take him to the operating room.'

"The nurse answered, 'But, doctor, we have so many and they need . . .' Then I started to scream. 'My husband before. First. Before everybody. I lost my daughter.'"

Three young men come into the Hadani home to find Joseph Hadani. They have just been to the hospital, where they visited Yosi Hochman.

Yosi Hochman and Joseph Hadani and the three young men in the small room of the apartment all are members of the Egged (bus cooperative) football team.

Hadani, his neck bent forward, rubs the stitches on his head meditatively while the three tell him about Hochman.

Hochman's wife and two children were killed in the attack. Hochman was wounded and lost a leg.

The three young men say that doctors at the Rambam hospital believe they can save Hochman's other leg.

"If he can learn to use it with a false one on the other side, he'll be all right," one of the young men says.

Hadani looks up at his three friends and says quietly, "Thank God."

□

"All I kept telling myself was, 'She still breathes,' and I waited outside the operating room in the hallway," said Mrs. Hadani.

"There was a man there, it was an Arab man. But a good Arab, you know? His wife was inside having a Caesarean and he was waiting for his child to be born.

"We smoked his cigarettes and all of a sudden I wanted to talk.

"I ask him, 'Are you a Jew?'

"He tells me, 'No, but I'm a human being . . .'

"He said, 'Don't be worried, there'll be good news. They will save her.'

"I knew it was only words, but I was glad to talk to him. I needed to talk."

"Then, the nurse opens the door and told the man his wife was all right. I cried, 'What about my daughter?'

"The nurse comes to me and holds my arm and says, 'She won't leave. We did what we could.'

"I didn't say anything. I couldn't. I went to find my husband. They had him with shots in bed, but he spoke through the medicine. 'What happened, what happened to her?'

"I held his hand and I told him, 'She's being treated. It's all right. Don't worry.' "

□

Now Ayelet tells her story. At 10, she has poise and she knows it. Her bright green eyes shine, her cheeks are pink with the excitement of the telling. The adults urge her on with pride.

Hers is the one triumph in the Hadani household. She escaped from the bus before the terrorists took it over.

Someone yelled to get down on the floor — many did and became hostages.

"But I didn't," she said. "I saw the back door was open and I ran."

She hid in the bushes on a nearby hill, found a friend, Danni, also 10, and led him back to the road to flag down a police car. She led the police to where some of the wounded were waiting for help.

She and the wounded were driven to a hospital in Hadera, where she was examined and pronounced fit.

"There were so many people," she said. "They took one man right from the door into the operating room. An old couple came and wanted to take care of me . . .

"Five minutes later, they released us and they took me to a restaurant. I told them I was a diabetic and they asked me if I knew when I had to eat. I decided to have some sugar so I wouldn't go into insulin shock.

"Mamma always told me to be brave. To be strong. Grandpa is very religious. He always told me to trust in God."

Then she showed a Donald Duck picture she had colored very neatly that day. And she told about the letters her 4th-grade classmates sent her Monday. One said she was like Steve Austin, the Six Million Dollar Man. Another boy wrote: "I want you to live for 500 years."

☐

"That night, Ayelet slept with me. I just told her (that) daddy and Na'ami were having treatment, that everything was all right," Mrs. Hadani said.

"Yesterday, the next morning, when we woke up, I gave her breakfast and then, in the kitchen, I took her hand and I said, 'If you promise to be strong, I'll tell you.'

"I told her, 'You may have to be sister to an invalid.' I wanted to tell her little by little. Nobody else should tell her. We understood each other. She might have heard it on the radio.

"Then she promised to be strong. I hugged her and we cried.

"I told her, 'Don't wait for her, little Ayelet. She won't come any more. But don't cry. I need you to help me. I need you to be strong.'

"Then we listened together to the radio. They were announcing the dead. The first name we heard was Na'ami. I was just happy that I told Ayelet before."

☐

Now Joseph and Levana Hadani have left the small room to take care of their guests. It is part of the shiva that they should do so, that they should be among the living.

Joseph's sister, Malka Meroz, remains in the small room. She leans back and sighs wearily.

"After the Sadat visit, we felt a little bit relaxed," she said. "We felt maybe the peace was coming to us. Now, it's a dream. It was too good a dream."

"Now the parents are every day guarding the kindergarten," said her husband, Michael.

"Something must happen," said Mrs. Meroz, leaning forward again.

"Something must happen — to them. Something dramatic, something to shock them, the Palestinians. Perhaps we must pay (back) in the same way. I don't think some Arab mother must cry, but something must happen. It is not heroism to kill children. The world must do something about it."

"Maybe the answer must be in the same way," said Itzhak Hadani. "I don't understand this killing of children in the middle of the day. But I don't know if I hate them. This will not bring me back my niece. I don't know if revenge is the answer."

Then from the corner, Moshe Kaski, 69, Levana Hadani's father, held out a hand and got silence in the room.

"I will say this and you will make a translation," he said.

"This is the Bible: We, the Jewish people, have to suffer all our lives and to sacrifice sometimes our lives, but those conditions bring us to be hard. And those who want to destroy us will themselves be destroyed."

And then he too rose to go out to the guests in the living room, and the telling of the story was over.

MARCH 17, 1978

RAS EL BAYADA, Occupied Lebanon — It is
eerily still in no-man's land, a two-mile testa-
ment to the lesson that people are as much a
part of the landscape as houses and fences and
fields.

Here, eight miles from Lebanon's southern border, between the last Fatah commando checkpoint and the spearhead of the ad-
vancing Israelis, the chickens come out to
meet you on the road. It has been 48 hours
since grain was scattered for them in their
yards.

Here, everything is frozen in time, like a
Pompeii without the lava. Crates of oranges
are stacked, unattended, next to empty
houses. Telephone wires dangle broken and
useless from their poles. An open spigot pours
an endless stream of water onto a swamp that
once was a garden.

Here, the mere whoosh of a breeze
through the leaves can make you sprint for
cover, scanning the sky for warplanes until
you dive into the orange groves . . . only to
emerge a moment later feeling foolish and
shaky from the rush of adrenalin.

To be sure, there is noise and plenty of it.
There are real planes and anti-aircraft guns
nearby. Artillery blasts thudding on the hill-
sides make the sheep bleat as they scatter and
the frogs wail in the ditches.

But it takes man's noise to break the
stillness — a child's cry, an engine or a laugh.
And without man, the eeriness is unrelieved
in this world between two worlds.

Behind the last Fatah checkpoint, the
teenagers bearing Kalashnikov submachine
guns and wearing jaunty red berets talk quietly among themselves for long, nervous
hours.

The fear of the Israelis is palpable. The sky is constantly watched. For 48 hours, on the streets and in the fields, the little bands have shifted.

They move constantly — occasionally fighting, more often just moving, farther and farther back.

The latest news is passed by word of mouth, from the children who seem to be everywhere, or from passing Jeeps or cabs full of commandos.

Transport is arranged on an ad-hoc basis. A Peugeot with no muffler stops. A Lebanese is driving. A Palestinian sits by his side. The back seat is stacked with 16 captured Israeli machine guns.

This is Fatahland, as the Israelis call it, where everyone might be a commando and children of 10 know how to handle the Kalashnikov.

Fatahland has been shoved north from the border, helter-skelter, so that now it is near the ancient Mediterranean port of Tyre. Still, the welter of movement and talk is quite organized.

There are few radios and no walkie-talkies. But the movements of an outsider — every step he takes — are watched and reported.

For two days, in the face of Israel's massive assault, the Palestinian forces have had to shoot and run away.

"There is no way for us to face such heavy weapons," said a commando officer in Tyre. "It would be useless. It would be foolish."

Still, on the village streets and in the camps along the coast, the spirit among the commandos is broodingly vengeful.

"With every step, they will pay," the officer said. "They will pay a price such as Israel never has had to pay."

The Fatah command posts have been moved and re-moved to avoid the threat of Israeli artillery and bombs. Yesterday's location was unknown to 12 of 13 commandos near the front. Yet, somehow, the orders get through. The communications network is the whole population.

Everywhere, but nowhere in particular, stand the young men with the light machine guns. When the first rumble of planes is heard, they silently slip away. After the last Israeli bomb has dropped, they are suddenly, miraculously everywhere again.

Close to the last Fatah checkpoint, the fear shows on every face. No one knows whether the Israelis will push forward again.

The civilians have begun to disappear. Cars and trucks full of refugees have been leaving for the last two days. One Mercedes heading north last night was filled with 16 people — three in the front, four children between the seats, five on the back seat and four sitting in the open trunk.

In the streets and fields, there is constant movement.

"You had better go away now," said a commando at a headquarters near Tyre. "It not good to stay too long in one place."

As the last checkpoint approaches, the taxi driver bows out. For once, it is not a matter of money.

"I am Arab," he says, and he draws a finger across his throat to indicate his fate on the other side of the line.

The commandos at the barrier are startled by footsteps. "It is impossible, don't go," they said. "The Israelis are very near. They kill for nothing."

And then, all is past, and the stillness sets in.

On the lone walk, there are monuments to the violence of 48 feral hours.

A BMW sedan with a flat tire is pulled to one side of the road. Except for the tire, the car is intact. There is no explanation for its presence, until a door is opened to reveal upholstery spattered with blood.

Farther along, five cars are burning. Their stink testifies to the accuracy of the Israeli aerial assault. The blistered hulks sit on bare wheels, tires burned off in the explosions that halted the cars.

In the back of a Mazda, a burnt skeleton of a machine gun lies in the open trunk. When the machine gun is moved, two lizards dart out of their new home for the bushes at the side of the road.

There are daisies growing in the bushes, and the air holds the scent of honeysuckle. Birds sing in the intervals between explosions on a hillside to the east.

Suddenly, around a bend, the squawk of a shortwave radio cuts through the air.

Ahead, two giant Israeli tanks stand on either side of the road, their snouts pointed toward Fatahland.

The tanks form a gate, of sorts, to a new world, one of pure geometry and punctilious organization. To the left and right, fields have been cleared of their crops and American-built personnel carriers scuttle over the raw earth on rubber treads.

There are halftracks and Jeeps, supply vehicles and trucks busy here and there.

The Israelis are settling in, bringing a new order.

A visitor causes some consternation. There is nothing in the manual.

"Go there," says a private atop one of the tanks. He points to a spot on the road, cutting off further questions.

"They don't let us talk," he says.

The Israeli equipment almost gleams. It is huge and new, as American as a baseball bat.

Communication here is by radio. There is no shouting, only the roar of machinery on the earth.

About 50 soldiers surround the machines. They pass without words. A couple of them gawk. One smiles.

In the middle of the field, a group on foot is listening to rock music on Israeli radio.

But there is worry on their faces, matching the fear on the Palestinian faces up the road.

"They are all around here," a freckled private says.

He looks west to an orange grove and the Mediterranean, only 150 yards away.

"I cannot tell you that there are not terrorists behind those trees right now."

14

Another complains that the personnel carriers are not armored.

"They are only aluminum," he says. "Even a regular bullet passes right through."

A third soldier cuts him off.

"Don't talk," he says.

A major pulls up in a Jeep. He has a printed itinerary taped to a band on his arm.

There is a discussion about whether the visitor should be forced to leave. No one can seem to imagine walking through the orange groves in Fatahland.

The major says the Israeli forces are going nowhere this day.

"If you ask me, I'm not the prime minister," he says, "but I'd say this is it."

Hebrew barks over the radio of his Jeep. He answers with a monosyllable and climbs back in.

"You will go back?" he asks, incredulous, with a look up the road.

"You are crazy."

MARCH 19, 1978

NABATIYE, Lebanon — From the door of the shelter, the two men can see the town being blasted to bits, block by block.

Houses, streets and shops disappear. When the smoke clears, there is only another square of garbage.

Shell after shell — perhaps 100 rounds — falls closer and closer, marching slowly up the hill toward the patio of the old stone villa under which the shelter was dug.

On the patio, near the shelter stairs, Sami is edgy. He takes a few steps, stops, looks toward the center of town, picks up his machine gun and puts it down again.

Sami is young, 21, he says, and he has been fighting for only three days. He is a Lebanese from the south, a lean, black-haired farm worker who took up arms only when the Israelis invaded Lebanon last week.

From the top step of the shelter, Shehabi, the other commando at the shelter door, tells Sami to get inside and settle down.

Shehabi is in his 30s. He carries a slight paunch as comfortably as he carries his rifle. He has been through many shellings in his six years with Al Fatah. "Take it easy," he tells Sami, "there's nothing you can do."

A far-off roar announces the approach of Israeli jets.

"Mirage," someone outside yells. "Everybody in. Down."

All scramble down the rough cement steps to the blackness below, in the heart of the hill.

The planes fly so high they are difficult to see. But the commandos insist that the air crews can see them on the ground if they move around in the open. So there are orders to stay underground, around the table littered with tea glasses and orange rinds, in the dank air that stinks of kerosene.

When the bombs hit, even though they are two-thirds of a mile away, the air in the shelter vibrates with a sound too low to hear. The glasses rattle. The talk stops.

When it starts again, the subject is how long the fight will go on.

Sami and Shehabi agree. "We will fight until they are finished," Sami says. "Out of the land."

Right now, for these two, there is no fighting to be done. The bombardment and shelling of this market town have lasted most of the day. The Israeli firepower is awesome. The invaders have emptied and smashed Nabatiye, at least for the moment, without setting foot within five miles of the town.

But the commandos are still here, in shelters like these, and Shehabi, the veteran, knows it is a victory of sorts.

"Look," he says, "you see what they can do. They may take this town, but how many times? How many soldiers do you think they will have to stay in all the towns?

"And for what?" he asks.

An artillery blast nearby fans the air of the shelter. "Look," Shehabi says, as if in rebuttal. "Here we are."

And for what?

They say in the shelters and orange groves of southern Lebanon that this will be a very long, bloody war.

Unless the Israelis withdraw, or gradually build the Lebanese Christian Phalangists into a force capable of holding the south, or adopt the U.S. plan of a neutral United Nations occupation force, Israelis will die every week.

So they say in the shelters, while the bombers hammer the earth. And sometimes, so saying, they laugh.

"Begin comes for revenge of (35) Jews in the bus and loses how many — 200, 300?" a young commando on a road near Tyre says, laughing. He tells his fellows: "We will send them teachers for arithmetic."

Of course, Israel's count of her war dead last week is much lower than that of the Palestinian command. Israel's own estimate is eleven.

Whatever the number, it is well known here that the death of a single Israeli soldier is an occasion for national mourning. That is an attitude on which the Palestinians hope to capitalize.

There is also no way to be sure of the number of Palestinian commandos killed in Israel's invasion. Here, too, the claims vary widely. The latest Israeli estimate is 200. The Palestine Liberation Organization says that is too high.

The commandos have been pushed away from Israel's northern frontier. From that point of view, the Israeli attack was a total success.

But in the south, a mile or two away from the new Israeli zone, it is clear that the Fatah commando brigades have not been broken, only pushed back.

And from conversations throughout the south, it is equally clear that the only guarantee of the security Israel seeks from the raids of the Fatah commandos is the death or capture of thousands of Palestinians.

"They can push, they can occupy, maybe the whole south, maybe the whole of Lebanon," a Fatah official says. "Most of our men are under orders to fire, to hit and then to escape. Why stand to fight? Why try to stop them? This is not the point. Not with the weapons they have.

"But nobody will give up, this is what you must understand. A battle is won or lost, but a revolution like ours goes on until victory. It will be a guerrilla war," he says.

"You have seen the orange groves in the south. There are no big highways, only little roads that go in valleys, around the hills, and the trees on both sides — you have seen it. How many RPGs (rocket propelled guns, anti-tank weapons) do you think we can put in those orange groves, you see?

"They will pay. They will pay every minute. A grenade from here, an RPG from here, a bullet from there. They will pay every minute."

Right now, it is the Palestinians and the Lebanese of the south who are paying the dearer price.

The destruction is tremendous, the disruption complete. The towns are emptied little by little, carload by carload as the shelling continues.

In the strip occupied by Israeli ground forces, six miles deep into Lebanon, the troops move in with armor, wary of the suicide squads that the Palestinians are said to have left behind.

When all is quiet, the houses still standing are searched one by one, each door kicked in, each cellar probed.

The refugees from the towns and Palestinian camps leave most of their belongings behind. They stream up the roads, in cars scraping the pavement, 10 people inside, mountains of household goods on top.

Still, after four days of fighting, the Palestinians have shown they can endure and regroup. Israeli settlements south of Lebanon have been shelled from behind the new Israeli lines. Single, furtive snipers walk in and out of the new border strip the Israelis have created.

And from the still-smoking towns, the commandos emerge, to flee, to join another band, to plan another mission.

In Nabatiye now, the bombardment has stopped, or perhaps just paused. No one is sure.

Cars race out of town at 80 miles an hour, down the narrow roads like the ones the Israelis will have to patrol.

Through town, the taxi driver dodges piles of rubble and wires that may still be live.

The road is rutted, and a Jeep has piled into a Peugeot ahead.

From the back seat, Shehabi tells the driver to slow down.

"You cannot outrun an airplane," he says.

A sheep has been run over just outside the town. The taximan misses the carcass by a foot. Behind, a Fiat runs over the sheep and skids to a halt in a field.

An old woman with a huge burlap bag on her head pleads by the side of the road for a ride. The cars whip past her at panic speed.

Shehabi tells the driver to let him off at a point on the coast road.

"I will stay tonight with my friend, if he is here," he says. "Oh, yes, I'll go back. Perhaps tomorrow, perhaps after tomorrow. But we will all go back."

MAY 23, 1978

CAIRO — Slowly, with pain, Orani Mahmaud Daker climbed the stairs to the second floor schoolroom where he was supposed to vote.

He propped himself with a stout wooden cane that was in his right hand. His grandson, Rashid, helped on the left. His breath came in short whooshes from brown cheeks, which were not so much wrinkled as folded where the absence of teeth let the skin go lax.

Once Orani Daker was a tall, graceful man. But 32 years delivering water in Cairo, a liter at a time from a heavy leather gourd that pressed cold and damp against his back for 10 hours a day, had stiffened and bent him and used him up before his time.

He looked as though he might not make it through the day.

But it was an important morning, a referendum day. He closed his cigaret stand in Babalouk, near the alley of the watersellers, and made the long walk through Cairo's crowds to do his duty for President Anwar Sadat. He would vote, provided God willed it.

He straightened with a sense of dignity and mission at the top of the stairs and moved toward the voting table with a shuffling step that swung the hem of his galabia gown just above the dusty floor.

At the table, a gaggle of police officers and teachers conscripted to be election workers fiddled with the ballots, drank tea, and smoked.

Daker inclined his head, in a clean white cloth wrapped into the shape of a tarboosh. "A lovely morning to you," he said, and handed the officials his voting card.

There was confusion. The officials searched for his name on their lists. Daker stood patiently, murmuring the 99 names of God. He was sent from one room to another, then back to the first.

Finally, a teacher found his name.

"Can you read?" he said.

"Yes," said Daker.

"Do it right, there are foreigners here," the official said, handing him a paper ballot.

"May the good God elongate your life," said Daker. Fitting a pencil into his right hand, perpetually closed as it was for so long over the strap of his heavy water bag, he carefully filled in the center of the red circle on the small slip of paper.

He thus voted Yes, to a series of propositions banning all kinds of putative undesirables from positions of power, formally consigning the press to a role as an arm of the

state, endorsing prosecution and penalties for anyone who is thought to have "jeopardized" social peace or national unity."

Daker took his cane back from his grandson and made his way to a chair near the top of the stairs, to rest. He said he had voted for Sadat.

"Any election, if it is for re-election of Sadat, I will go; if it is for Nasser, I will go; if it is for the men in the People's Assembly . . .

"God will bring into power whoever is good," he said. "Democracy is right, 100 percent."

□

Democracy was at work all over Egypt Sunday, as 11 million voters were asked to fill in a red or a black circle — answering Yes or No — at more than 23,000 polling places.

The results were announced yesterday: 98.29 percent of the nation's voters favored the six referendum points enunciated by Sadat one week earlier.

No one would say so as the voting went on, of course, but there had been a strong hunch even before the polls opened Sunday that the results would turn out something like that.

Democracy has not been present here long — scarcely more than 20 years. But in that short time, it has established something of a pattern.

The pattern began, as did so much else, with Gamal Abdel Nasser. He and his fellow "free officers" of the Egyptian Army seized power and overthrew King Farouk in 1952.

In 1956, when the Republic of Egypt was established, Nasser won the nation's first presidential election with 99.9 percent of the vote. In a nation with 5.5 million voters, moreover, only 178 failed to show up to affirm Nasser's "nomination" as chief executive.

Sadat took office with a slightly less spectacular performance. After Nasser's death in 1970, only 91 percent of the Egyptian public affirmed Sadat's "nomination" as successor.

By 1972, Sadat's ideas apparently had caught on. A lengthy new constitution published for the first time on the night of Sept. 9 was "affirmed" in a referendum two days later by 99.98 percent of the eligible voters.

By 1976, Sadat was able to go Nasser one better, obtaining from the voters a 99.93 percent affirmation of his "nomination" for a second term. Only confirmed pessimists took note of the drop in voter turnout — 3 percent of the voters stayed away.

There is an easy explanation for Egypt's high voter turnouts: a law fining any registered male who fails to vote. Females, registered in relatively small numbers, are not obliged to vote.

The electorate's remarkable unanimity is partially explained by the form of elections. In Egyptian presidential elections, for example, one does not choose among several candidates. There is a single presidential candidate, and one votes Yes or No.

In Sunday's referendum, the questions at issue spelled political doom and possibly prison for several groups identified by Sadat as possible "corrupters" of the political process.

But, as only one Yes or No was required from the voter, there was no way to distinguish between, say, those who corrupted the political process in the days of the monarchy before 1952 and those who may be corrupting politics or upsetting the social peace now.

"No matter," said Ahmed el Atar, 59, a pharmaceutical inspector among the early voters at the school in Babalouk.

"We agree with everything the president says. Yes," he said. "We say Yes."

Muhammed Abd el Naib, 38, a teacher of English at the Ibrahim T. E. Mustafa Kamel Preparatory School, who was helping to administer the election at the Babalouk school, reported proudly that nobody had voted "No" all day.

"Until now, nobody votes No, but, you know, every country has good people and bad people," he said. "'Bad' — 'No.' 'Good' — 'Yes,'" he giggled.

"You know our President Sadat," he said. "Perfect in all his works."

□

On his chair near the landing, Orani Daker was launching into his own encomiums in praise of Sadat.

"You see, now we have insurances. We have now pensions," he said.

He felt in the pocket of his galabia with his twisted right hand and produced a limp paper, folded several times. He opened it with near-reverence, taking care not to tear the paper along the folds.

Like many of his age and class in Cairo, Daker will not customarily talk to an honored stranger about whether they had voted. "What is the point?" said one young man. He estimated that 80 percent of the students would have voted No, but that only the other 20 percent voted.

Cairo University's campus, just across the Nile from the center of town, was unusually quiet. Perhaps by coincidence, the referendum occurred in the midst of the university exam period, minimizing political concerns on the part of the huge student body.

The most excitable of the quadrangles, that of the faculty of engineering, was closed to unauthorized persons. The secret police at the gatehouse explained that it had been closed since a fire of suspicious origin wrecked a new building two weeks ago. Then a superior came to explain that it was closed so that students should not be disturbed during examinations.

These days, Cairo University is not the only place where fear and politics tend to go together.

There is a new police presence throughout the capital. The leftist newspaper has been banned and a wave of political arrests has chilled political discussion.

The message came from Sadat one week before the referendum, when he said of his political detractors: "I will crush them with democracy."

No one knows how far the crushing process will go.

The Helwan University students said they believe that only the leaders of opposition parties actually will be threatened. A leader of the opposition leftists said he thinks that the crackdown is aimed at "anyone who raises his head to speak."

There is no doubt, though, that Sadat's tough words, the referendum and the hints of political repression that already have surfaced herald a period of introspection.

It may be an inevitable aftermath of disappointment over the stalled peace initiative with Israel, an initiative that had carried such a burden of hopes for Sadat and all Egyptians.

It may be the same impulse to introspection that made Israel's 30th anniversary earlier this month so somber an affair.

□

The police officer had been standing there all along, as Orani Daker had praised Sadat, as he had talked about his son and showed his insurance papers.

Something stiffened in the officer's back and, when Naib, the English teacher, joined him, the air of the little circle around Daker at the top of the stairs grew sour and apprehensive.

Daker's talk had passed from politics to life. He had grown expansive in the warm sunshine streaming through the window, in the fragrance of the tea that someone brought, in the joy of talking to strange young men who wanted very much to listen.

"Even if water and civilization now reach most of my houses," he was saying, "I still know them. I knew them — may the Lord protect and defend them — when they were little children and used to beg me for a drink from my — excuse me — spout. Now they are big men — doctors and engineers, some of them. I made a good population."

From somewhere behind the office in the front row another voice complained, "His profession is disgraceful."

The English teacher complained to the highest-ranking policeman, "They will write that Egypt is underdeveloped. Get that old goat out of here."

The mood at the top of the stairs grew hostile. Daker felt it, and started folding his papers, having problems in his haste with his stiff right hand.

He called to his grandson and stood, in pain, to make the long walk back to business. As fast as he could, he made for the top stair.

"Get moving and see that you keep your mouth shut," said the officer. Daker looked as if he had been slapped.

On the street, minutes later, his listeners caught up with the old man shuffling slowly through the dust and traffic.

Daker smiled ruefully at the invitation to a cafe.

"No, I was finished," he said quietly, looking down. "It doesn't matter so much."

He and his grandson walked off slowly through the noon heat, toward the alley of the watersellers.

OCTOBER 11, 1978

BEIRUT — There was the little girl with freckles on her nose and a startling red rim of blood under the iris of her left eye, looking for a still younger sister who had disappeared.

There was the 55-year-old woman, crying like a schoolgirl as the empty tanker truck pulled away toward the west, leaving her, empty pail in hand, without any water for the third straight day.

There was the family on adjoining beds in the corridor of an East Beirut hospital: the boy with hands thickly wrapped to cover the burns from a phosphorus bomb; the girl with the gauze-swaddled head rolling slowly from side to side on her back, moaning, "ay, ay . . . ay"; the mother, still, kept flat on her back by the tubes running in and out of her nostrils, dumbly following with haunted eyes the movement of faces above; and next to her, the bed where the father lay until dawn yesterday when they covered his face and quietly carried him out of the hallway.

All the horror of Lebanon's war is back in the tight, once stylish hillside streets of East Beirut.

The cease-fire called during the weekend stopped the pounding of heavy guns, but it revealed for the first time the full fury of the Syrian assault on the Christian quarter of the city.

For nine straight days, the Syrians poured everything they had onto the rolling blocks of apartment houses and shops. The bombardment was not totally indiscriminate. All but one bakery suffered direct hits. The water pumps and reservoir for the quarter were hit often and destroyed. Hospitals received more than their fair share.

The fighting between the Christians and the Syrians has used all the tools of a modern war on the streets of a crowded city, as if Pennsylvania's national guard had assembled all its heaviest pieces atop the Penn Center towers and systematically set out to destroy the Art Museum area.

One shell from a 240-millimeter mortar hit the apartment house at 33 Rue Antoine

Khoor, in the Asherafiye section, at 11 a.m. Saturday, just nine hours before the cease-fire took hold.

A 240-millimeter mortar shell is a missile of steel almost five feet long. It weighs 233 pounds.

When the shell came in the front of the 10-year-old concrete building, it shattered the front wall of the first floor entryway, where a couple with the family name of Saier were sitting against an interior wall.

The woman, whose age was estimated to be 60, was thrown into a corner and partially buried by a hail of plaster and glass shards. Her neck was broken and she died.

The man, said to be slightly older, suffered a crushed arm and a broken leg. Doctors will check for spinal damage when there is time.

The shell continued through the entryway into a rear basement, where it smashed into the roof of a makeshift concrete-block shelter erected by the family Abi Saad. George and Joseph Abi Saad, their wives and their children, 14 people in all, had lived in the shelter for a week.

The roof and walls of the shelter caved in on the family when the shell hit. Two dead members of the family were discovered five minutes later, when neighbors burrowed in and found them. Ten others died later. George Abi Saad and Joseph's eldest daughter, Josephine, are still alive in hospitals.

□

When the shell hit the shelter, it flew apart, scattering bits of steel jagged enough to cut through a man like a knife through soft cheese. Of the 70 to 80 persons in the basement, about 20 were hurt badly enough by shell fragments or debris to require hospitalization.

Some, like Nicola Emteini, were lucky enough to escape with something minor: a cement chunk that flew into his face, scraping it raw and breaking his nose but sparing his eyes and skull. Luckier still, Emteini, 13, blacked out when the shell came through.

"I just saw the shelter explode in my eyes. I don't know, I'm trying to remember," he said.

"I hope he never remembers," said a neighbor who was there.

More than 10,000 rounds from mortars, heavy cannon, rockets and grenade launchers fell in East Beirut last week.

Those who stayed and survived — there was no choice but to stay since the Syrians closed the roads out of town — and emerged from their shelters Sunday, had a hunted look about them.

East Beirut is short on sleep. Everyone is running on nerves. The Phalangist fighters, screaming up the glass-strewn streets in their hot-wired cars, slow warily, one hand on the guns at their sides, to inspect each passerby on the street.

The old men sitting out of sight, just inside their ruined apartment buildings, jump when someone speaks to them. Shopkeepers who still have merchandise sit watch on their counters 24 hours a day behind their locked steel gratings.

It is the material shortages that hurt right now. The Christian quarters of the city, the most stylish neighborhoods in the Mideast last month, now are down to the animal needs.

Pretty women in their thin, strappy sandals and monogrammed designer shirts, fought each other yesterday to get at a flow from an unsanitary water spring that runs through the subbasement of an office building here.

A water tanker on a mercy run in a street only 10 blocks from well-supplied West Beirut had to pull away by force from the crowd that scrabbled at its rear taps, yanking the hoses from clutching hands and racing down the street.

A single bakery that opened its doors spawned a line that ran to the end of the block. Customers were limited to six loaves and offered anything to buy more.

Near the front of the line stood a red bearded man of fighting age who had, nevertheless, none of the swagger of the militiamen in his quiet carriage and demeanor. George Rizk, 24, said he is a mathematician, or rather, was when things were good. "Now," he said with a rueful smile, "I work at buying bread. Two hours so far. After this? Then I will wait for water."

□

Electricity went weeks ago. Candles now are gone. Communication is by rumor, or by Phalangist Radio, an arm of the militia. A three-day-old newspaper is highly prized, a three-day-old banana even more so.

At hospitals, everything is short. The Lebanese Hospital, one of three in East Beirut, was a 15-year-old building for 150 beds. Now it is a wreck.

More than 100 shells came into the hospital. All patients were evacuated, two and three at a time, whenever it seemed safe. Yesterday, in the one hallway judged to be secure, five beds were lined up ready for new victims.

The kitchen was shattered, the generators smashed, the laboratory took two hits and the operating theater all but disappeared. The ambulance burned up when it was hit. Twelve nurses were injured during

the week. Others got hysterical and became patients themselves.

John Kalache, 32, an orthopedic surgeon who spent 10 straight days in the building, displayed the new operating room in an administrative office, the new electric lines he and a resident had strung from the emergency generator, the new walls made of filing cabinets padded with mattresses.

Kalache, who trained at New York's Lennox Hill Hospital, said the Lebanese Hospital was a target!

"Look at the buildings around — intact. None of them got what we did. They had to be trying," he said.

He said two of his patients were out of danger when a shell came through a window into the room where they lay.

"One died there. The other, we operated. He bled to death. And those were two we'd saved."

Then he hurried off to look at the hospital's newest case, a Lebanese army lieutenant, shot in the back by a sniper.

At the St. Georges Hospital, the 250 beds were made to hold 700 last week. Now, the load is down to 350. Most of the beds stand in the halls. Rooms with windows were mostly destroyed.

In the courtyards, stinking fires of stained dressings burn throughout the day in an effort to keep a semblance of sanitation. But infection is spreading fast.

In the hallways, food trays and empty cans lie under the beds. Families have moved in to be near their wounded. They have no where else to go. Mattresses lie inches apart on the bare floor of a room that was once supposed to be an amphitheater. For some there is no linen.

In a janitor's closet off one corridor, the naked, shriveled forms of two old patients lie on bare mattresses. Only their rattling breaths reveal that they still live. In the gloom of the close, airless room, they look like corpses thrust aside to rot.

"We have no place for them," a nurse said. "They have cranial tumors. They were in Intensive Care. Then, Intensive Care received two shells."

□

The ones who got to the hospital are lucky, said Dr. J. A. Shaheen.

"Most of my patients can't get in," said Shaheen, 35, a kidney specialist. "They can't get here for dialysis. They are dying. I will lose half of them."

Shaheen was trained in Boston and Rochester, N. Y. He has a job waiting in America whenever he chooses to go. He said he is not going — not like this.

"I might have gone before the shelling, but after, I will stay. They will not force me out of here. I am a part of these people now."

And, he added grimly, "This is not over."

"This is just a temporary pause," Shaheen said. "There can be no peace with them, after this kind of misery."

It is the bleakest revelation of all from a tour of East Beirut. No one is cleaning or repairing. Everyone is waiting for the guns to start again.

Like Josef Shouhry, 48, who was asked why he continued to climb over a pile of debris to get into his apartment building. "Why should I spend my time?" he asked. "Nothing is finished. Nothing has changed."

Like Rizk, the mathematician, standing in the bakery line. "Like all men here, I must stay," he said. "The women and little children, O.K., they can go out. But when the men leave, we are finished, they have won. And we are not finished yet."

Or like the long-haired girl who finally found her boyfriend, lying on a makeshift bed tucked into the X-ray room of the St. Georges Hospital.

Thick gauze pads covered the wound where a shell fragment had ripped into his abdomen on Friday. A respirator device bobbed up and down on his glottis amid a welter of tubes.

She picked up his limp hand and said, "Tony, Tony . . ." and looked in vain at his face for a flicker of consciousness.

"Tony, oh Tony," she said, and bent to kiss his hand. Then, bent double over his hand, crying onto it and kissing it again and again, she said quietly, urgently, "Tony, it's not over, Tony. Tony, it's not over, do you hear?"

NOTES AND COMMENTS

The telephone company reaped a windfall profit as a result of our interviews with Richard Ben Cramer. We wanted him to talk about his powerfully written stories out of the Middle East. Three trans-Atlantic phone calls—one a very long one—did the trick. But it wasn't easy. Cramer had been to Rhodesia, backtracked to Ireland, stopped off in London, zipped down to Basque country, and was about to hustle off again to the Middle East.

In very rickety English a hotel clerk in Bilbao, Spain, explained that we had just missed him. Finally, we found him in his London flat, struggling with his expense accounts. "My table is covered with receipts in 17 different currencies, and the accountants in Philadelphia are getting ticked off."

Cramer described his London digs, the place from which he covers Europe, Africa and the Middle East for the *Philadelphia Inquirer*: "I'm sitting here in my own flat. It's a large Victorian room. Unfortunately, it had to be rented furnished. It's done in neo-Iranian with tassles hanging off the couches."

During his brief but spectacular tenure as a foreign correspondent, young Cramer has been robbed in Cairo, censored in Tel Aviv, spied on in Damascus and encouraged not to return to Kuwait. While covering the Israeli invasion of south Lebanon, he walked across two miles of no-man's land between the Israeli army and the Fatah commandos. They thought he was crazy.

Cramer's prose is as inventive as his reporting, and he consistently astonishes his editors—even with his memos. He once cabled a request for "two Hohner harmonicas, Keys D and F, Blues Harp model (not Marine Band)." To satisfy his curious editors he explained: "Well, I guess the truth must out. When I'm lonely, sad and blue, missing the hamburgers and drive-ins, missing the Miracle Miles and the girls in bluejeans, missing, I should add, all the warmth of *The Inquirer* city room with the soft cluck-

cluck of the staff, nothing seems to satisfy like boarding a felucca for a leisurely sail down the Nile, blowing mournful tunes through my little harp and watching the Arabs' Mercedes being smashed up on the coastal drive."

Consider the following features in Cramer's writing:

Strength of reporting — Cramer gets to where the action is, even at personal risk. The reporting gives him the detailed description, the personal sketches, the quotations and anecdotes that bring the stories to life.

Sensitivity toward people — Cramer's characters are fully developed, complex in their humanity. The writer clearly has a feel for the rhythms of life in foreign places and an ear for the cadence of language.

Striking images — Within a single, well-balanced sentence Cramer can create an image that tells us much about the devastating effects of war on a civilized people: "Pretty women in their thin, strappy sandals and monogrammed designer shirts fought each other yesterday to get at a flow from an unsanitary water spring that runs through the subbasement of an office building here."

Varying sentence length for dramatic effect "When the bombs hit, even though they are two-thirds of a mile away, the air in the shelter vibrates with a sound too low to hear. The glasses rattle. The talk stops."

Placing the reader in the middle of the action "The fighting between the Christians and the Syrians has used all the tools of a modern war on the streets of a crowded city, as if Pennsylvania's National Guard had assembled all its heaviest pieces atop the Penn Center towers and systematically set out to destroy the Art Museum area."

Using a natural setting to create a mood and a sense of place — "Here, the mere whoosh of a breeze through the leaves can make you sprint for cover, scanning the sky for warplanes until you dive into the orange groves ... only to emerge a moment later feeling foolish and shaky from the rush of adrenaline."

Symbolic structure — The story out of Haifa begins with the funeral of a nine-year-old Jewish girl killed in a Palestinian commando raid. It ends with an old Jewish man giving a Biblical lesson on the suffering of the Jewish people. At the heart of the story is a Jewish mother who waits in a hospital for her child to die. She is consoled by a "good Arab" who waits for his child to be born.

In our telephone conversation Cramer talked at length about his writing and his reporting experiences even though the connection occasionally sounded like Marconi's wireless. We also talked with Cramer's editor for these stories, James Naughton, now Metropolitan Editor of *The Inquirer*.

Interview with Roy Clark and Richard Ben Cramer

CLARK: These stories won many awards. Why were they so well received?

CRAMER: Two things. First, the execution of the stories all depends on meeting individual people who are there and who are in it. I must confess I was never a great reader of foreign news. I figured out last year that I never read it because I never got a sense of the people who were caught in it. When you meet an Egyptian man whose whole life has been taken up fighting the Israelis with whom he can think of no legitimate quarrel, it makes it intelligible in the gut instead of the head. And that's a whole other way of writing foreign news. The second thing is the *Inquir-*

er's philosophy of reporting. We don't try to give the day to day political back and forth. We try to step back from the situation and give a different view. To do that the *Inquirer* is willing to send a bozo like me around the world for a year at tremendous expense and give me a lot of space in the paper. If the editors like the story as what they call a "read" — which is not grammatical, but eloquent in its own way — they'll get it in the paper if they have to trim everything else in sight. Really that's heroic editing.

How do you involve people in your stories?

Well I think the process is really in the reporting. Take a simple example. Say there is a fight going on between Christian Lebanese in Beirut and the Syrians. To anyone sitting in Beirut this is an easily intelligible situation. The overview is readily available. You call up the Christian command and ask what their casualties are, and you get the Syrian pronunciamento on the same subject and you put down the conflicting claims and explain the political background which led to the most recent clash. You get a different story if you get into the neighborhood that has been bombarded and go to the people who have been shelled out of their homes. You keep in mind that these are people who are affected in the same way you or your readers might be in that situation. Then you find yourself more interested in how this event has changed their lives. That's far better than the casualty figure school of reporting. It's a question of what you can get. It's very easy to take the conventional wisdom about what is happening. It's usually much muddier but much more interesting if you have the whole welter of detail that a bomb creates, if you will.

Sometimes your reporting actually puts you in the middle of the event, puts you in danger.

At times, yes, but not as often as some people would like to think. That's sort of important. You know its very hard to know what someone would feel in a situation unless you at least feel something of it yourself. It certainly helps to put yourself in the other man's shoes if you are an inch and a half from those shoes.

I get a sense of balance from the whole series, the war from many different perspectives.

Basically my nightmare is the sound of newspapers being folded up and thrown on the floor all over Philadelphia, so what I try to do is keep the reader involved in the story. And if I'm in a region for a year, I'm going to hit just about every point of view because I think that's more interesting to people than the same one over and over.

In the story about the bombing of Beirut, you compare the situation to a hypothetical one in Philadelphia. What were you trying to do there?

I was trying to show what it looked like. When I think of bombs exploding, I think of them coming over long distances — I think of five mile cannon. This was something different. This attack was basically like shooting fish in a barrel. I wanted my readers to be able to know how close those Syrian gunners were and how direct the attack was. I would have liked to have been able to talk to the Syrians about the feeling of shooting at a building with a 50mm cannon when you're close enough to that building to see into the windows.

You use many concrete images that tell a larger story — the freckled girl with the rim of blood under her eye, the women in fashionable dress struggling over unsanitary water. Did you look consciously for these?

One of the lovely things about reporting in the Middle East is that you're never short of shocking images. When you're covering something that vicious, that takes place in that beautiful setting, you don't really have to look too far for images that mirror a larger situation.

You spend time describing the natural world and even give the reaction of sheep and frogs to the bombing and devastation.

Can I tell you a charming story? I have a friend on the *Baltimore Sun,* my first newspaper, a guy named John Bainbridge. He read that story about how the bombs make the sheep bleat and the frogs wail. And I got this cable from him saying "Frogs wail? I know you misquoted people, but now you're misquoting animals!"

What stylistic values do you bring to your writing?

Like any reporter I'm trying to get a lead that gives some sense of what's going on while not causing that hated sound of papers being folded up and thrown on the floor in boredom or disgust. My great problem is getting out of the lead and into what the *Inquirer* calls the nut graph. Some papers call it the hoo-hah, the paragraph that tells us why we are doing that story. I've always had great trouble with this. My editor during the Middle East trip was a guy named Jim Naughton, a guy with a very firm hoo-hah indeed. He occasionally put in a nut graph or ordered me to put one in.

Why do you feel uncomfortable with giving the reader the reason for doing the story?

I like to tell the story of the people, to describe the place, to give a sense of how it feels. It seems a little presumptuous to tell the reader what you're going to demonstrate to him. It seems to foreclose some of the reader's options. One man's nut graph may be false to another man. If two readers are coming out with different conclusions from my observations, then they're bringing to the process of the article something active. They are creating, along with their newspaper, which I think is good. The more actively they read, the better I like it. My other great problem is that I'm an overwriter. If I have the time, I let the story cool for a few hours — go back and read it as cool as I can. I take anything out that makes me say "Come on! Give me a break!"

When you write do you think about the structure and the rhythms of your sentences?

That's exactly what I'm thinking about. I know how the sentence should sound to me. And events themselves have rhythm. Moreover, stories have rhythm and if you change your rhythm badly or if you put in a jumble of different rhythms you lose something of the reader's interest and creative participation. What I do is walk around these hotel rooms, reading the stuff to myself, reading it out loud sometimes, and then I sit back down and tug out some more of my beard and rewrite it.

The story out of Haifa — the one that begins with the family sitting shiva over a dead girl — has a remarkable organization. For example, it begins with the funeral of a young girl and ends with a lesson about suffering from an old man.

Some stories just write themselves in the sense of structure. I have to explain how that story was done. I was in Egypt when the attack on the bus took place. I did not get the news of that bus attack for more than 24 hours. So when I heard it, I went berserk. I was in terrible shape and my poor Egyptian interpreter really caught it. We went racing around trying to get from Egypt to Israel. I got to Tel Aviv the evening of the next day, two days after the event. I learn of this family outside Haifa, but I didn't know how hard it would be to get there. I had to pay a taxi driver a hell of a lot of money to drop me up there in the rain and just sit there waiting for me. He brought me down to a hotel in Haifa where I tried to write the story by Telex, but they wouldn't send it without a censor seeing it. I was trying to write and trying to wake the censor up to read it. I can't tell too much about how the story was structured because it was written in a kind of white heat of frustration.

The most stunning anecdote in the story is told by the Jewish mother in the hospital waiting room, being consoled by the Arab. She is waiting for her daughter to die. He is waiting for his child to be born.

Wasn't that nice? When I heard that she had talked with an Arab man and then when she said it was a "good" Arab I knew this would be the centerpiece for the story. Because at that moment, while her child was dying, for her to have to recognize that they were not all murderous Arabs — there is something quintessentially Israeli and sad and difficult in that.

Interview with Jim Naughton

What makes Cramer so good?

JIM NAUGHTON: He's one of the best writers I've ever encountered in journalism. He's got an eye for detail, an ear for meter and lifestyles and the way people talk that is phenomenal. He is equally good at reporting and writing.

What is the secret of his success in writing foreign news?

What he does is write about real flesh and blood human beings instead of nameless, faceless governments. There is a trap, a very seductive trap, for national and foreign correspondents and particularly for people who work in places like Washington to write stories in which the lead says "the White House announced yesterday" or "France said yesterday." It's insane. What Cramer did was to set out and consciously write about people, to find the people lurking behind the institutions, the people affected by governmental policies. Most of what he did was to cover events such as the movement toward peace in the Middle East, from the perspective of people who would be the beneficiaries of the search for peace. I think we don't do enough of that, not just in foreign coverage, but in all journalism.

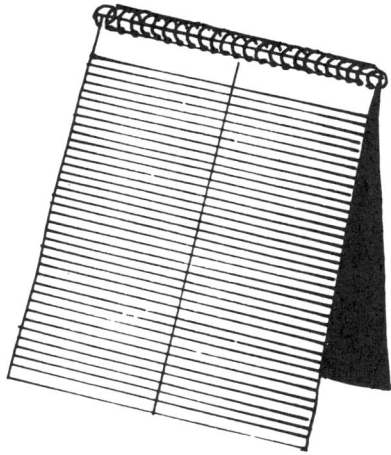

Diane Torelli

EDITOR'S NOTE: Mary Ellen Corbett has been a journalist for more than 20 years, working on newspapers and magazines in Illinois, California, Hawaii and Massachusetts. In 1974 she began a weekly syndicated column on women's issues, "Feminist Q & A." She continued the column for four years, travelling the country to lecture on "sexism in the media." On New Year's Eve 1977, Ms. Corbett was informed that her ex-husband, Harold Corbett, had crashed his plane off the coast of Hawaii. Hal and Mary Ellen had married in 1967 and divorced in 1973, but remained close friends. After Corbett's heroic ordeal and dramatic rescue, Ms. Corbett spent several days interviewing Hal about his experience. She wrote an 11,000 word series on the subject, which appeared in more than 100 American newspapers. She now lives in Brandon, Vermont, and is writing a book about Hal's ordeal at sea.

Mary Ellen Corbett was sponsored in the ASNE competition by the Fort Wayne (Indiana) News-Sentinel, an afternoon paper with a circulation of more than 72,000.

1979
Prize Winner
Features

Mary Ellen Corbett

It was New Year's Eve in the shark-inhabited waters off Hawaii's Kona Coast, and Hal Corbett was preparing to die.

Only minutes earlier, his single-engine Piper Cherokee Arrow, with two passengers and a dog, had crashed into the Pacific, three miles short of the runway, while coming in for a landing at Keahole Airport.

Ocean depth at point of impact was approximately 3,000 feet. The time was around 7 p.m. — twilight.

The pilot, Harold Corbett, 49, of Honolulu, slid out of the sinking cockpit and reached his wife, Dianne, 44, and their year-old cocker spaniel, treading frantically in the blackening night.

There was no sign of the other passenger, James Specter, 36, a visitor from Denver,

Colo., who had arrived in Honolulu only that afternoon to look into investment possibilities in the islands.

Not a single lifejacket, seat cushion or fragment of wreckage remained afloat.

Corbett, owner of a Honolulu flight school, and his passengers were on a 90-minute flight from Honolulu International Airport to the Big Island — in good spirits and looking forward to that night's New Year's Eve Party with Corbett's relatives and friends at Kona. The lights of the shoreline and the brightly illuminated runway stretched before them as they made their descent. Everything was going perfectly until Corbett reduced the power setting in his preparations for landing.

"Then," he says, his voice breaking, "there was a loud snap. The plane went into unbelievable vibration. We were at about 600 feet, vibrating like we were on a paint shaker."

The plane was doing 85 miles an hour when it smashed into the sea. First, it slammed flat and Corbett thought they'd made it all right. But before the first impact had fully registered in his brain, the plane bounced, pitched forward and went in again, this time nose-down in the ocean.

Dianne and the dog, Mandy, apparently were hurled forward over Corbett, in the right front seat, and over Specter, sitting front left. Evidently the intensity of the second impact threw them clear of the aircraft.

Corbett heaved forward, head crushed between his knees. He felt a searing pain in his skull, but saw or heard nothing in the seconds after impact.

"I had the sensation that water was all around me, and I was afraid to take a deep breath for fear I'd suck water into my lungs.

'I've got to get air if I'm to help the others; I thought to myself, reaching to unhook my seatbelt."

He rolled to his right in the darkness, feeling for the door that wasn't there. Then he realized that he was in the water, and he stroked his way to the top, noting as he did so the plane's still-lit taillight sinking quickly into the water beside him.

"I knew for certain then that the plane was lost. Specter had vanished," Corbett said.

"Honey," he heard his wife call out as he broke the surface... "Honey, I'm over here."

"It took me about five seconds to swim to Dianne. My first words were 'Are you hurt?' "

"No, I'm okay," she replied, with amazing strength in her voice. And then, "Honey, I can't swim!"

Corbett kicked off his shoes as he answered her: "Here, hold onto my shoulder. Don't worry, we don't have to swim anywhere. We just have to tread water."

"Oh, Lord, help us! Oh, Lord, save us!" Dianne cried in the darkness, her arm moving from her husband's shoulder to encircle his neck. "How long will it be before someone can help us, honey?"

Hal choked as he answered, because Dianne clung so tightly: "About a couple of hours, probably."

"I can never make it."

Then their little black puppy swam up, and with what sounded like joy in her voice, his wife said: "Honey, Mandy's with us. Mandy's here, honey."

"Yes, I see her," he said, pushing the animal away from them after unhooking her heavy leash and chain.

He was struggling to keep himself and his wife afloat while trying to get out of his slacks.

"You've got to get rid of your clothes," he told Dianne slowly and deliberately. Each word was a labored effort. He was already exhausted and fighting for air.

Somehow she managed to rip away her blouse. Hal went under, holding his breath, to undo her heavy, skintight jeans.

There was discouraging frustration for him in those next few seconds. As his air supply dwindled, he was being pushed deeper and deeper into the water by his wife. He couldn't, though her life seemed to depend on it, unfasten or tear loose Dianne's complicated belt. "I guess it was then I knew - I had my first instinct, that we were in very serious trouble."

He swam back to the surface, strangling, working to hold them both up.

"You've got to let go for a moment, so I can breathe," he gasped in barely audible tones. "Okay, honey," she responded, only slightly releasing her clutch.

Once he got a gulp of air he told her to take hold of his shoulder again. He was desperately treading water now to hold them both above the surface.

Instead, Dianne gripped his neck from behind and again his air was cut off. He sunk below the surface a second time, to try to pull off her jeans. Then he went even deeper, forcing himself away from her. He came up at arm's length, coughing, choking and fighting for breath. He knew he had to hurry to her, as she paddled for her life.

"Here, hold onto my shoulder," and she clutched at him once more. His gasping started almost instantly, and he choked out his words: "You've got to let me breathe."

"Okay, honey" she called, but held on.

"You've got... to... let... go... so... I... can... breathe," he gasped, thinking he couldn't hold them up much longer.

"Okay, honey," he heard her say again, but he knew she hadn't released her grip.

With that he quit kicking, swam below the surface and put his hands under her arms to push her higher out of the water. Then he let go of her and pushed away, again coming up alongside. He was struggling for just a breath of air, trying to remove his T-shirt, trying to clear his lungs, and to stay afloat so he could get back to Dianne.

He found he could neither speak nor breathe as he gagged to clear his lungs. He was battling to stay afloat.

"Honey, I can't hold on," came her words through the darkness. Another breath and he might have the strength to go to her. And then... "Honey... I'm... going..."

He was frantic to reach her again. He felt suffocated. Seconds passed with no sound at all. He strained his ears for any sound. He reached out blindly, gasping. But there was only stillness. Dianne was gone. The dog was gone. Had she taken hold of her puppy as she went down?

When he finally heard something, he realized it was the moan of his own weeping.

"Yes, then I thought 'It's my turn,' " Corbett said, reliving those agonizing moments after Dianne went under.

"The desolation seemed too much to bear. I felt I couldn't take it. I was gasping for breath and thrashing in the water, thinking, 'Now I must go, too.' So many thoughts came rushing to my mind. I was trying to figure out about the crash and I was wondering how to go about the actual act of dying. It just seemed like something pulling me under.

"Should I just let my arms go limp at my sides and sink? I knew that I wanted to face the spot where I thought Dianne had gone under. I was still listening for her voice... I needed to hear her voice... but I knew that she was gone. I guess maybe I thought I could find her and be with her underneath.

"I was praying then, but it was a desperate sort of thing — words spoken but without much love or understanding. Most everyone, in times of panic, prays in purely selfish terms, I guess. Not until much later did I say my genuine prayers.

"But at the same time I felt I was beginning to get my air. My swimming was less helpless flailing. I was amazed to be able to get air in my lungs and I began to half-think, 'Maybe I don't have to go for a minute or two yet.'"

"I got my wind and twisted around in the water. There were the lights of the Kona shoreline. I could make out the lights of the airport. It was a greater distance than I'd ever negotiated in the water, maybe the length of two 10,000-foot runways. But something said, 'It's not so far, maybe I can make it.'

"Within five minutes I felt in complete control. Within 15, I realized that maybe I could hold on for an hour or two."

Corbett was treading water with determination now, doing mental calculations. He could tell by his view of the airport lights and rotating beacon before him, 60 feet above sea level, that he was approximately three miles out. He wanted to stay in the area where the plane had crashed, knowing the tower operator, who'd given him landing clearance, would send rescue vessels there.

"I knew it was New Year's Eve, and some pilots would be drinking. Those who had would not be able to search for me. I knew the holiday meant limited Coast Guard crews, and I forced myself to accept the wait of two to two and one-half hours. I knew it would be a good two hours before a boat or helicopter could possibly get to me.

"I knew I had to do different types of strokes — the hands-over-head swimming was much too tiring. First I did a dog paddle with a scissor kick, taking the work force off my right knee. Within six to eight minutes these muscles would give out and I'd have to do a side stroke, using my best arm and best leg.

"The salt water felt like it was burning my eyes out of the sockets, but I couldn't keep them closed because I'd lose sense of direction.

"I had visions of a nice, restful float position, or maybe an easy back stroke, but the waves were much too strong. I got water in my eyes, nose and mouth when I tried those positions."

Self-discipline was nothing new to Corbett, a 20,000-hour pilot who had been flying for 31 years.

This was his first air tragedy, but in 1967 he had been in a near-fatal traffic accident in Torrance, Calif. After that he had forced himself to do continual physical therapy exercises for many months in order to walk again.

Corbett's motorcycle had piled into the back of a car making an unexpected stop. He shattered both ankles, with compound fractures in both legs, a cracked tailbone, a broken right wrist, and fractured vertebrae in his neck — 50 breaks in all. His left hand had been severed at the wrist, but was saved through surgery.

They said he might never walk again or have the use of his left hand. He felt he could. And that's how he felt now.

"I set a goal of 30 strokes per minute, allowing occasional brief rest pauses. I had ruled out trying to make it to the shore at that point. I felt it was most important just to stay within the search area."

Corbett's thoughts were interrupted about 9 p.m. when he spotted the first search helicopter.

"The minute I knew the searchers were at work, all my attention was directed at them. I talked to them aloud, telling them how to find me in the water.

The first Coast Guard helicopter, dispatched from Barber's Point, Honolulu, was searching in a two-mile area much farther out than where Corbett was.

"Then the helicopter went back to shore, and I was sure he'd gone to refuel. I thought to myself 'Well, they probably won't be able to find a key to the fuel pump.' And that's exactly what happened! Then the pilot resumed his search with what remaining fuel he had. They eventually called him back in, I understand, having located a fuel man. But when they unlocked the pump to refuel, I was told, they discovered the nozzle wouldn't fit the helicopter.

"I began feeling the search was futile, and I knew I might have to be in the water all night. I was tired and cold and seemed to be hedging on my goals, and I was kind of resting in the water.

"There was no real pattern to my swimming then and that's probably what caused the sharks to first notice me.

Corbett said his first thought about sharks came only when the sharks arrived, about 9:45 p.m. "I'd figured I could just swim and rest. It never once occurred to me that I was lost in one of the most famous deep-sea fishing spots on earth! And where there are fish there are always predators.

"I had been resting when it happened, just sort of relaxing my legs in the water. Then I felt the pressure on the lower calf of my left leg as I stroked the water with my back to the shore.

"There was absolutely no question! A shark! I felt the length of him go over my leg, pressing with a firm pressure of eight to 10 pounds. I guessed it to be about six to seven feet long. Seconds later it or another one went by, in the opposite direction, same pressure on the other leg, two to three feet of its rough body rubbing carefully against me. I knew he was testing, measuring how alive or dead I was.

"A few seconds later it grabbed my right foot! I felt its mouth and the pressure of its teeth, covering all my toes for one second.

"Then, as it opened wider, to move over the ball of my foot like it was going for a bigger bite, I guess I began mentally reacting to the first nibble. I yanked my foot out, tearing my sock and pulling it part-way off.

"I shoved my head below the surface, yelling 'Aaaah, aaaah!' as I moved 360 degrees. I knew from my years of skin diving and taking underwater movies that loud noise will scare sharks — they really are great cowards.

"I came up for air and went under again, shouting in four directions. At the same time I started a firm swim, knowing I shouldn't create a splash that would frenzy the shark toward what he'd assume was a thrashing, injured prey. For the first time it also occurred to me that my crash injuries were perhaps bleeding to attract sharks.

"I was positive that I didn't have the strength to swim underwater, so I went to the next best choice, a strong dog paddle and scissor kick, yelling 'Help! Help!' above the water as I went. I hollered probably a dozen times so my voice might continue to scare the sharks, and in hope that maybe someone in a boat somewhere out there might hear me.

"A minute or two after I'd started swimming, the fright hit me. It was confusion. Overwhelming confusion. I was crying. I just couldn't understand what was happening. From all my diving experiences, I should have anticipated shark attacks yet they came as a complete shock. I felt terror and disorientation.

"That's when I really began a communication with God. I just kept saying out loud, in the dark: 'Lord, I don't understand. Why did I survive the crash and these hours in the water only now to be eaten by sharks?'

"I wasn't exactly complaining to God, I just desperately needed to understand. After about three minutes my fear subsided some and my head began to clear. I still didn't understand why I'd come to this point, but I knew some answer would come. I had the distinct impression that I was facing some tests and that I had to take care of myself.

"I thought how badly I'd feel if nobody knew I'd survived the crash and the hours since, to be killed by sharks. Also, I had so wanted it known that the cause of the crash had been mechanical, not a pilot error.

"I even thought of giving up at that point. I was tired and it would have been so simple. But the thought came back so strong in my head, that giving up would be a form of suicide."

Even desperate as he was, the idea of suicide repelled him. Corbett had been a churchgoer and a person with strong religious convictions all of his life.

He had been a member of many church study groups, and after his 1967 motorcycle accident, friends in Southern California's South Bay had set up round-the-clock prayer watches to plead for his recovery. Ever since his recuperation, a bout with a blood clot in his lung and subsequent bone surgeries, Corbett had been convinced, as were many people who knew him, that a miracle had spared his life. He was not one to doubt the probability of miracles — and his faith would not now let him give up.

"After my talk with God, I set another goal — midnight. I had to hold on until 12. I also knew I could no longer indulge myself with long rests of 60 seconds at a time. They could be only brief intervals, 15- to 20-second pauses, between vigorous swims. Idleness could bring back the sharks."

A short time later, a big search plane came.

"I could tell by the drone that it was a multi-engine. There were blinding search-lights in the aft underbelly, shining back behind, the lights sweeping with movements of the plane.

"I was elated. 'Six sweeps and he'll have me!' I thought to myself. I began talking to him aloud."

But the search plane made a pass and a half and headed in to Kona. Corbett didn't understand why he'd quit. He later learned that the plane had had engine problems, so the pilot turned back.

A small helicopter searched the shoreline, flying above the boats. There was no pattern to this flying either, it seemed to Corbett; no grid, just random swings. He could sometimes hear the copter's engine as he continued his endless swimming.

His mind was drifting as he watched the helicopter in the distance. Perhaps he hadn't meant to, but he'd been allowing himself to rest again.

"I was treading in the water and somehow a sixth-grade story popped into my mind. I remembered tales of sailors falling from ships and being carried to shore by dolphins. I smiled to myself and said: ' Hold it, Hal. This is no time for pipedreams. Now is a time for the possible, not the impossible.' Still, my mind went back to the dolphins — and I sort of rolled over in the water.

"Now, I thought in a vague sort of fantasy, if dolphins came along I would put out my arms like this — and let them carry me to shore."

He felt a twinge of silliness then, like he would not have wanted anyone to see him doing that. But still he stretched both arms out, cupping his hands as he might if reaching for a dolphin fin. It wasn't a practical swim position, so he told himself he was only trying to break the monotony.

After about 10 minutes, Corbett was relaxed and almost limp in the water. He had perfected a rest technique in which he would let his arms rest at his sides, expending the minimum movement to hold himself up and bend his head back, stretching his face and neck to keep them above the swells. His feet were almost in fetal arrangement as he floated vertically, one foot atop the other, as if perched on a shelf.

So at ease was he, at that point, that he was totally unprepared for: WHOMP! An upward force pushed him about a foot out of the water! It had been a smooth surface, like a 2-by-12 plank, slamming heavy on the soles of both feet.

He hadn't needed any warning to go into a determined swim. "Sharks!" his mind called out in terror. And he heard his own voice, again shouting for help.

"I began a strong swim for shore, calling for help after yelling again under the surface. It wasn't until much later, when I was well away from the area of the attack, that I took the time to try to figure out what might have happened.

"I was then aware of a little whistle or screech. I heard it again and more distinctly as screeching noises and splashing began near me in the water. Suddenly I knew it was Pacific porpoises — dolphins — discussing among themselves this human interloper in their midst.

"My God," I thought in that instant. "Was it dolphins saving me from the sharks?" Then I almost felt a need for laughter, for I knew that porpoises and sharks are mortal enemies and that the sharks would be scared away.

"Not until days later did I piece it all together. Now I knew the 'whomp' had been a dolphin. Even those dolphins had been an answer to my inner prayers.

"About half hour or so after the 'whomping' incident, I began talking again with God. I knew the Lord had to send me some sort of help if I was to go on all night.

"Lord,' I remember saying, and I was really sobbing then. 'Lord, I'm getting so fatigued and I need strength to keep going.' Then I had a strong urge to get into my calm rest position, and it came then. God's energy came."

"Once I realized that I could call upon God and get answers and instant help, I felt I should only ask for reasonable things. I didn't want God to think I was childish. I wanted only to ask for sensible things.

Corbett said it was about 11:30 p.m. when he began steadily thinking of the New Year's fireworks. He and Dianne had been on Kona the year before, New Year's Eve, so he knew from what direction the public spectacle would begin. Somehow it seemed so vital that he not miss the fireworks. He needed that absolute time reference to get him through the night.

By this time Corbett had adjusted to his environment and was learning to cope with the pain, loneliness and fear. He had adopted

a definite sort of plan to avoid any more en-
counters with sharks. He was perfecting his
rest technique, but now limited himself to
only a few seconds of rest at any given time.

Even elimination had become roûtine. He
handled the problems of urination and bowel movements with scientific precision. He
took special pains about cleaning himself and
quickly swimming away, before there was a
chance of waste matter attracting predators.

He had decided to keep his jocky shorts
out of a sense of modesty. Also, he knew that if
the sun got too hot next morning, the under-
wear could be used as a cap to protect his
head. He also felt the white fabric could come
in handy as a flag.

The socks he termed "invaluable."

"If a shark got me, I'd need a tourniquet.
And sagging off my feet as they were, I felt a
shark might take hold of the stocking material before it would get my feet. Also, somehow, the dark socks against white legs made
me feel that perhaps I looked more like fish
than flesh."

His pilot's wristwatch, a year-old Christmas gift from Dianne, was big and he thought
of dumping it. "Still, something told me to
keep it. I worried about the weight, yet I knew
I could use it as a signaling device in the sunlight. And the sharp cutting edge of the band
was a potential weapon. I thought, too, that it
would be so good, when the sun finally came
up, to be able to know the exact time. So I kept
my watch and my wedding ring. They made
me feel more secure."

The New Year's arrival was a milestone in Corbett's ordeal. And he wept aloud when midnight came.

"I saw the colored starbursts and heard the booms and I thought of the people on shore. Not just the people who knew we had crashed. But the strangers who were celebrating —just as Di and I had done last year. These midnight fireworks gave me such a link with humanity. And I was keenly aware then of my loss of Dianne, and the other passenger.

"One amazing thing was how the moon came up while the fireworks were under way. For a moment I even thought it was part of the sky show, until it lit up the slopes of Mauna Kea and Mauna Lea.

"I was so thankful that it came into view just at midnight, because it was so friendly, like a giant lunar timepiece come to acquaint me with the hour. I knew that it moved in increments of 15 degrees per hour, so my midnight companion would keep me posted on the time throughout the rest of the night.

"It may sound funny, but there were times, during the next few hours, when I wouldn't let myself look at the moon for awhile. I'd force myself to swim further and further before I'd permit another glance. I just didn't want to be a clock-watcher. It seemed so important for me to keep working.

"I was aware of a lot of little things against my body, and I knew they were probably small fish. I didn't get scared about that although I was concerned about encountering jellyfish."

One, in the moonlight, Corbett said he thought he saw an owl pass over him and he remembered that the Hawaiians considered

that a good omen. Then he thought briefly of his dear friend, Hawaii historian Inez Ashdown, who had told him of such things.

"There were lots of random thoughts as I swam. Some too private to repeat. And they came in jumbled order, with Dianne creeping back into my mind again and again.

"I remembered how, at the scene of the crash, I had thought of our privacy. She had always wanted us to work a little less, to have more time alone together. After she went down, and often through the next few hours, I pondered about how much time I would allow myself — in the future — for peace, meditation, recreation, rest. And once I had a glimpse of my messy office, recalling how I'd left it so disorganized, thinking I'll clean it when I get back."

Sometimes, Corbett said, he permitted himself little lapses of projection, when he'd think about swimming to shore and going to find help. After the shark attacks he had strong visions of a helicopter hovering directly over him, lowering a basket and plucking him from the sea. But even as he thought about that sort of rescue, he knew it was wishful thinking.

"Then there were constant longings for some kind of flotation, and I'd keep looking over my right shoulder, thinking some bouyant object would come floating by. I never did get over this sensation and occasionally I'd think about my little pillow Dianne would toss to me when I was watching TV at home, on the floor. I so needed that little pillow. For bouyancy, of course, and for comfort. There were moments when I greatly needed comfort.

"I was doing more vomiting and gagging as the night progressed. I'd ingest salt water, throw up and immediately feel better. After awhile the vomiting became as much a part of my routine as cleaning my eyes.

"It was like a constant cupful of salt water being tossed in my face. I'd take my right hand out of the water, still treading with my left — which was in great pain. I'd shake my hand to remove as much water as possible, then I'd use my index finger to wipe my upper eyelids. The stinging was fierce, nettlesharp, and after my fingers got shriveled from so many hours in the water, it became harder and harder to clear my eyes.

"I was aware of my broken teeth, but they gave me no pain. The only other constant problem was that triangular piece of lip that kept hanging down in my mouth. I just hoped it could be saved and later stitched up, so I kept pressing it firmly and trying to keep my mouth shut."

One of Corbett's most amazing recollections is his mental coping with the abyss. "I have always loved the ocean," he recalls. "I've surfed it, swam it, snorkled in it, dived in it, fished it, photographed it, tape-recorded it, boated in it, and flown over it. The only fear I've ever had was of what divers call the 'deep blue', the very deep water. It's a common fear, except for the most experienced divers.

"Always, on my dive trips off Baja and in Florida, when anyone would holler 'Shark!' we'd all jump in the water with our cameras. You see, I didn't fear sharks or the waves. It was just that deep, deep water. One hundred feet was the deepest I'd ever gone. That night I guess I reasoned it out that 'It doesn't matter how deep it is here, it's just water, at all depths.' "

Along about 1 a.m., the sharks came again. There was still nearly uncontrollable fear. Corbett felt a scrape of rough surface passing against his ankle. He began a strong swim toward shore, yelling as he went, watching a fin directly before him in the swells.

"I figured this one was about six or seven feet also, and he was moving at a good clip ahead of me. I yelled and yelled and continued swimming — and I was aware soon that he had gone. I knew that the only way I could continue to survive these attacks was to keep moving, moving, all through the night.

"That's when I prayed again, I asked God if it was physically possible to keep moving constantly all night long, yet I knew I had to do it. I resolved then that I could never rest more than 10 seconds per minute, and never again could I linger one or two minutes in one spot."

In the next couple of hours there was a discouraging chop to the water. No predators

64

came, and Corbett had lots of thoughts. There
were some shiny porpoise rolls in the water
during that period, too, and he was never sure
whether he saw waves or dolphins' backs.

His view of the airport was too blurred for
pinpoint accuracy, but he felt he was at least
staying within the area of the crash, so that
searchers might locate him at daybreak.

"I thought of my brother, Jack, at Kona,
and knew he'd be organizing rescue operations. And I thought of my Pop, who died last
summer. I remembered a lot about his plane
crash off the coast of Santa Barbara, in the
early 1950s, and I tried hard to think of what
he'd be doing in my situation. And I had
taught him to fly. I knew also that I would
need him to help me get going again.

"Now I was still a couple of miles from
shore and about three miles south of the point
of impact. I was trying to get nearer the beach
with a vertical-body swim, which didn't seem
very effective. Instead of increased effort at
this point I lapsed into what I considered an
'existence swim.' I knew what I had to do to
keep from drifting out. I knew what I couldn't
do since the chop was picking up.

"I wouldn't let myself glance at the moon
more than every 45 minutes or so. I was perfecting my rest technique and I felt sharp
pains in the left side of my chest — which, I realize now, were the fractured ribs. At the
time, I thought maybe I was overtaxing my
heart. So I would try to slow myself down to
take the burden off my heart.

"Once I remembered what my Mom used
to tell me as a child: 'The Lord never sends
more than we can handle,' but things seem to
be getting harder and harder to handle.'"

"This was a really strong time in my communication with God. I had a 10-or-20 minute conversation in which I sobbed out my desperation.

"My chest felt like it opened up again and I got a tremendous surge of power. It was like someone filling me with warmth and it poured into my whole body. Then it closed.

"I said 'No, God! That's not enough! I need more! I must have more power!'

"And, like the miracle it was, my chest opened a second time and this time the energy just filled me until I felt as strong as I had at the moment of the crash. My whole body eased. I had inner confidence and renewed hope. And all this at the time seemed normal to me.

"At the same time I realized that the chop had gone. The water had calmed. I got everything I asked for."

For the next three hours, until about 7 a.m., Corbett maintained a steady swim pace, alternating strokes so he never got overly tired in any one position. He did some serious thinking about ground-rescue problems and found himself wondering what they'd be planning on the shore. He was trying to maintain a position in the area where fishing boats would be trolling at sun-up.

By 5:30 a.m. he realized he had lost all gains and had drifted two miles further south. He felt he had depleted at least 80 percent of his existing energy. He began to cry and felt he was at a breaking point. He called out to God, asking for the waves to calm again. Within minutes, he recalls, the waves subsided.

"I had really looked forward to sunrise, and it seemed like it would be a spectacular sight after the long black night. All I'd seen in the way of light through the past few hours was the shoreline and little jagged paths of light on the water, where the moon and stars were reflecting down. Suddenly, there was the sun, but it was diffused, almost like a small bare lightbulb. I was a little disappointed.

"Daybreak also brought a sort of mirage. I got up on a wave and was looking to the shore, wishing I could find some really calm water. I could see a really smooth area, it almost looked glassy. Well, with brighter daylight and better visibility, I realized this glassy area had really been nothing more than a construction zone at the shore. I laughed for a second, thinking, 'Oh, that's a joke on me.'

"I was glad when it got light enough to check my watch for time. I was amazed to see that I had been only a few minutes off on what my concept of time had been.

"In the period just before daybreak, I'd been calling out for help every 20 or 30 minutes. I'd call four times, in all directions, wait a minute, then repeat my calls. This way, if some fisherman had heard me, and was straining to hear again, he could be sure with my second call.

"This calling out had been exhausting, and once it got light, I quit it. I knew then I only had to call out when I could see a vessel coming. Also, I didn't feel the acute need, in daylight, to shout to scare off sharks.

"At about 7 a.m. it was like punching my mental time clock. I thought to myself: 'Okay, time to get to work.'

"And about that time my plan crystalized. I was rapidly talking to myself: 'I'm approximately four miles off shore. My goal is to make two miles in the next three hours. I will have to average one and one-half miles an hour. I'll swim at least 55 minutes of each hour, resting about 30 seconds every five minutes or so.'

"It was like a realization that it wasn't fair to wait for rescue. I had to do it myself. At this point I gave up all dependence on anybody on shore. I felt I had to do it alone.

"This was probably the most exciting time for me. I got into a rest position and said: 'Okay, Lord. I'm ready. Send me power!'

"And there wasn't any doubt that it would come, as it had before. The power flowed in then. I just closed my eyes and felt it filling me. I knew then I could do it. And I began.

"I swam with a vigor I can't explain. And yet at the time it seemed absolutely natural. I remember watching a house on the shore, seeing its details gradually loom larger."

He knew that at about daybreak a fixed-wing aircraft or helicopter could begin searching for him. His hopes were getting up.

At 7:15 a.m., there was enough light, plenty of visibility, but no searchers were in sight.

At about 7:45 a.m. a helicopter went well out beyond him, searching five miles north of his location and working in the opposite direction.

And around 9:30 a.m. a 28-foot fishing boat came trolling within three-quarters of a mile of him, paralleling the beach.

From 8 to 11 a.m. there were three large fishing boats a mile beyond him in the water. At the shoreline a small plane flew in a practice holding pattern.

Away in the distance, other boats headed toward a well-known tourist attraction, the historic City of Refuge, up the coast from Kona. But nothing came close to Corbett.

About 10 a.m., after his three-hour vigorous swim, Corbett remembers a cigarette butt floating past him.

"It was silly, but I felt a link with people, and I just stared at it in the waves. I thought 'How can I use it?' Finally I watched it to measure my tread in the water and to gauge the current at that time."

At 11:15 a.m. Corbett came to the conclusion that he might be able to last through the day, until evening, but he was certain he couldn't survive another night at sea.

"I guess I was thinking about my future then, too, feeling there is so much undone, wondering 'What is it I'm to do with my life?' I wondered the lesson to be learned from all that had happened and I knew in time it would come.

"I guess in that time span I also realized how often I had despaired. At times I contemplated suicide, when I felt my strongest despair. I heard a voice talking to me then, telling me not to give up.

"By now the day was really warm and I wanted the sun at my back so passing boats would have a better sense of color and definition about what they could see in the water. My swim procedure was holding but not making much headway, and a few times I tried signaling passing boats with my watch. It was off my arm only eight or nine minutes, I think, but then I couldn't force it back on.

"One boat came by during this period and I signaled, flashing my watch in the sunlight, as he came within a 45-degree angle of me. Then I signaled again at 90 degrees and at 45 degrees of his leaving. Then, as a safeguard, I did some waving with one arm, but it was very painful to do this, because of my injured wrist.

"I almost laughed at my own pathetic watch signals, because I knew how little chance there was to be seen.

"Shortly, I forced my watch back onto my swollen arm and began swimming again.

"It was getting near noon now and I felt the sun beating down directly overhead. I realized I was being carried further out to sea. I was losing all the gains of that three-hour swim. I was drifting out of the boat traffic area and I had a sense of crucial timing. I tried to ride the swells and I was calculating the long, long time I'd already been in the water.

"When another boat passed, I still had not lost faith. I had waved as he went by me, thinking, 'Just perchance someone may see me, maybe even some little child will see my arm in the water.'

"As the boat went out of sight, I told myself 'That's okay, he'll be back at the end of his trolling run, in an hour or two. I'll get him on his way back home.' And my confidence still seemed strong.

"Maybe I'll have to wait until late afternoon. I guess I'd better get closer to shore."

Corbett started swimming again, with resignation. He turned his body in the water and took about three or four firm strokes before looking up.

When he raised his eyes out of the swells, he blinked at the most incredible sight of his

49 years. Directly ahead of him, barreling down with proportions that seemed like the Queen Mary, was a 42-foot sport fishing boat. People were gaping over the side, waving, and he knew that he was safe.

"I started crying in the water. 'Thank God. Thank you, God.' And I just sobbed as they cut their speed and opened up a gangway to let me crawl aboard."

Weeping as he relived it, Corbett said: "You know, nobody on that boat saw me when it passed — except for one little boy, who thought he'd seen a man's hand in the water. After he repeated what he'd seen to a fisherman on board, the captain was alerted and they did an immediate turnaround.

"I don't remember much that was done or said. I was bleeding once I was on deck. Someone tried to cover me with a jacket. I refused it because I just didn't want to get blood on anybody's clothing. And I asked for a diet soda. I don't think anything has ever tasted better to me than the first cool sip.

"People on the boat stayed way back. I guess I looked pretty bad. I asked somebody for a mirror, but they said I couldn't look at myself. Once I thought I saw the boy who had spotted me in the water. But when I looked again, he wasn't there. And I closed my eyes, and cried."

Corbett's rescue boat, the *Humdinger*, had been chartered for the day by Beverly Hills attorney Walter Weiss and his wife, Municipal Court Judge Jacqueline Weiss, and their sons, Andrew, 10, and Jack, 13.

"Jack spotted something first," Weiss said, "and he asked the skipper, who dismissed it as a coconut. About that time I came up on deck and saw something too. It looked like a man's head and arm. I said 'That's a

man!' and the skipper responded, 'My God, that must be the pilot who crashed.'

"The first thing he said when we got him on board was 'Thank you!' I have never seen a guy with more guts. It was incredible. He was smiling but looked terrible. His body was bloody and his whole scalp was covered with blood. His jaw was awry and his mouth was bleeding with broken teeth hanging out.

"To be honest, he looked unreal. He looked like a creature of the sea, not a man, all white and wrinkled.

"After about 10 minutes he took on a little color and began to look more like a human being. But my boys were afraid. They were crying. We all just looked at amazement at this battered man who was talking — and smiling.

"We all felt something very special happened that day."

Once in the harbor, an ambulance took Corbett to the hospital at Kona. His 12-noon rescue on New Year's Day was an astounding 17 hours after the crash. He had drifted more than 12 miles from the point of impact, but his long fight with the ocean current had been successful — he was still only three miles out from shore.

At the hospital he was treated for shock, exposure and loss of blood. His body was covered with reddish-purple bruises. His voice was weak and raspy from yelling and the constant irritation of salt water. The flesh under both arms was worn away, leaving ugly, weeping sores. His 5-foot-9 and one-half inch frame had lost 10 pounds of body weight, from 199 to 189.

"They took X-rays at Kona. I didn't know there were any breaks. But I was in such pain. That's why I knew I had to get to specialists once I was back in Honolulu.

"I could hardly walk because of the muscle soreness and pain in my limbs and body. The subsequent examinations and X-rays turned up fractured ribs, fractured hand and knee. They put a splint on my leg, treated a deep gash between my fingers, and put me on antibiotics to fight infection which had begun to fester around my shark wounds.

"My dentist did preliminary work to repair my broken teeth."

That patched up his body, but what of his emotions? Is there a moral to the story of the man who survived that ordeal? Corbett says there are many morals — and that in time, even more will come.

"I have some very personal realizations," Corbett says. "And I know that if Dianne and I could relive our last three years, I'd give her more of my time. And I'd try to reinforce the identity she so badly wanted for herself. I guess I'd try to make her appreciate herself as much as I appreciate her.

"The most remarkable thing I've come away with is faith — the sheer asking and receiving. I know now that God is just waiting to be asked. It's there and I'm going to tap that source.

"And I think I've learned that no matter what we're doing, be it work or even survival, we just should never give up. The answers can and do come."

NOTES AND COMMENTS

A famous book about a man lost at sea begins "Call me Ishmael," which lacks the five Ws, and would probably be changed by a modern newspaper editor to "Call me, Ishmael said Thursday."

Mary Ellen Corbett begins her "lost at sea" saga with a more conventional news lead: "It was New Year's Eve in the shark-inhabited waters off Hawaii's Kona Coast, and Hal Corbett was preparing to die." Melville would have liked it. With all its news information, it still packs the power of the opening line of a good short story.

Unlike a writer of fiction, a journalist is wed to the facts. Hal Corbett did not, after all, crash his plane on Flag Day in an Iowa lake inhabited by guppies. Fate gave Mary Ellen Corbett the opportunity to write a narrative with significant time (New Year's Eve), an exotic setting (Hawaii), and a dramatic plot (a man struggling in shark-infested waters).

But stories do not really write themselves. A writer with a sense of story takes full advantage of the facts, selects some for emphasis, shapes them, arranges them and gives them life. Mary Ellen Corbett's lead does this so effectively, it deserves closer scrutiny:

Significant time —— By introducing the time element in her lead, Corbett follows standard reporting practice. But the time means more here. The lead sets up the ironic and symbolic implications of New Year's Eve, explored throughout the story. The irony is that the celebration on shore hampers the rescue, but is also an important time marker for Hal, and has the effect of lifting his spirits. Without making a symbol a cymbal, the writer takes advantage of the common associations of the New Year's ritual: the spirit of renewal, death and rebirth, the passing of the old order.

Exotic setting — People enjoy reading adventures set in faraway places. In this case, Corbett uses her knowledge of the Kona coast to create a sense of place and to give a full picture of Hal's predicament.

Jaws — Just when you thought it was safe to go back into the water, another movie comes along to convince you that the deep is full of ravenous monsters. Sharks. Hal Corbett's harrowing encounter with sharks is central to his adventure, and the writer wisely chooses to entice us with sharks in the lead.

Sentence structure — For the record, Corbett's lead is a compound sentence, with two independent clauses. This permits her to balance the introductory facts with the dramatic second clause.

Placing emphatic words in a sentence at the end — That exemplary principle is from Strunk & White's *The Elements of Style*. By ending the lead "and Hal Corbett was preparing to *die*," the writer places the most emphatic, and dramatic, word in the lead at the end.

There are many other things to admire in Mary Ellen Corbett's writing:

Stylistic detachment — Although personally involved in the story, Ms. Corbett never refers to herself, never intrudes into the narrative. Yet she writes with a compassionate voice, sympathetic to her ex-husband's traumatic loss.

Weaving facts into the narrative — Corbett includes hard facts about air speed, time, water-depth and distance without disturbing the flow of the story.

Creative punctuation — " 'You've got. . . to. . . let. . . go. . . so. . . I. . . can. . . breathe,' he gasped, thinking he couldn't hold them up much longer."

Perspective that gives visual power to description — "When he raised his eyes out of the swells, he blinked at the most incredible sight of his 49 years. Directly ahead of him, barreling down with proportions that seemed like the *Queen Mary*, was a 42-foot sport fishing boat. People were gaping over the side, waving, and he knew that he was safe."

In a telephone conversation from her home in Vermont, Mary Ellen Corbett told the fascinating story of how she became involved in this article and how she came to write it. On the line was her husband, Lewis A. Little, of United Features Syndicate. Little helped edit the story.

Interview with Roy Clark, Mary Ellen Corbett and Lewis Little.

CLARK: How did you come to write this story?

CORBETT: First off, the man the story is about, Harold Corbett, is my ex-husband, and a very close friend. When he was lost at sea I was notified by his family, and when he was rescued, one of the things he asked for was that I come to him. When I arrived in Hawaii, I wasn't really thinking in terms of writing. I was thinking of going to help a friend who was going through a very traumatic thing. But once I got to talking with Hal, I realized there was a powerful story and I knew I had to get it down on paper. That's just a reporter's instinct, I guess. Once I started talking to Hal, I decided it was important that I take notes and that I not wait for his memories to fade. I interviewed him everywhere — in his house, in the car, while he was getting X-rays. We spent about 100 hours taking notes.

Was telling the story therapeutic for him?

Hal needed very much to talk about it. He made it very easy for me. He probably would not have opened up as he did for another reporter. He realized the therapeutic value of getting all of this out. We are close friends. He trusted me to sift out the things that might be too tragic or too personal. I had an advantage. It just rolled out of him. He trusted me, so he didn't weigh anything in terms of how it would sound in print.

Wasn't being so close to the story a disadvantage too?

It was a disadvantage because it made me privy to a lot of important information. Some of it was shattering and it made me weep as I wrote it down. The objectivity question nagged me. I was involved in the tragedy because I loved this man, his grief was my grief. Once the story started to unfold I realized it was the biggest thing I had ever covered. I wanted to do it well. And I began to realize that doing it well meant eliminating some really touching things. For instance, Hal talks in the story about a voice that he heard encouraging him in the water. He said that was my voice. Well I had to decide how to handle that. In the end I decided to take myself out of the story in those cases. Maybe in this story I was on the alert and was trying very hard to establish a style that was objective. People would recognize that a reporter had sifted through all this material. Somewhere along the line I decided that this story needed a staccato approach. I felt it had to keep moving and that the short, quick description fit well because I wove them in with a lot of quotes from Hal. I recognized immediately that I had these wonderful quotes, so it seemed like the less I involved myself in the story, the more I let the story tell itself, the better it was going to sound.

You not only tell the story of this man's adventure at sea, but you deal with his interior, spiritual life as well.

The "miracle" aspect was something I had to weigh. It seemed obviously a miracle to me. Here was a man who was overweight, he was out of shape, he had a broken back, a broken hand, a broken knee, a possible concussion, he had just watched his wife die, and yet he had this ability to swim 17 hours without flotation. That to me seemed totally miraculous and yet how was an editor going to react? Was it going to sound like testimony at a tent revival? In the end I decided we couldn't weigh that. We had to write it like it happened and let the editors and readers judge. As it turned out, editors weren't offended by the spiritual aspect, and the readers loved it.

Let's talk about the lead: "It was New Year's Eve in the shark-inhabited waters off Hawaii's Kona Coast, and Hal Corbett was preparing to die."

I wasn't crazy about the lead. I thought that this story called for a much more beautiful kind of lead. But I knew it was going to be a long account and I felt if I wanted to hook the reader but good, I had to get in the basic news elements in the lead. So I went with reporting training and got all these things in the beginning.

LEWIS LITTLE: Remember you had written a couple of other leads, Mary Ellen, that just didn't work. They were too long and you would not have gotten the suspense that you were able to get if you hadn't put down the basic facts at the beginning.

CORBETT: After two false starts Lew said to me: Look, pretend that you're a reporter. Be direct, try to eliminate the personal ties, keep it simple, and start over. And on the third try, once I got the lead, I found that I was writing it faster that Lew could edit it, and I wrote it in one sitting, from about 10 in the morning until 5 or 6 that evening. We didn't stop for meals or anything. Once I started going on it, it was like I had this story in my head and it was screaming to get out.

You get New Year's Eve in the lead. Were you conscious of the irony that this tragedy was occurring when most people are celebrating?

Absolutely, absolutely. It seemed that created a mood from the beginning. If it had been December 27, it just wouldn't have had the same impact. Later, when we get to the part where Hal sees the fireworks off the Kona coast, I was able to work out some of the ironic twists.

How about the symbolic associations with New Year's Eve. The spirit of rebirth and renewal?

Absolutely. This is something that I bring out more in my book — I'm now working on a book on the same subject because of all the personal aspects I couldn't cover in a newspaper treatment. The symbolism of New Year's is big in the book.

The lead also introduces an exotic setting — Hawaii — which would be naturally interesting to the reader.

I felt that added a lot. I tried to tell people about the Kona coast of Hawaii, to bring some things about the island into the story.

What about the Jaws element: the shark-inhabited waters?

I started out with *shark-infested* because it seemed to have so much drama to me. We took it to Phil Reed (Phillip G. Reed, former managing editor of International News Service). His immediate reaction was: *shark-infested* is trite. He urged me to leave out the sharks. But in this case, I felt the sharks were an important element for hooking the reader. But I changed it to *shark-inhabited*.

Of course you save the most dramatic clause —"and Hal Corbett was preparing to die" — for the end.

LITTLE: Somewhere along the line, Mary Ellen, you played with the phrase "and his whole world had collapsed around him." Then you came up with the more dramatic one.

CLARK: You took 100 hours of notes. How were you able to organize that material into a coherent story?

CORBETT: Hal's recollections were coming in streams of consciousness. So I ended up with hundreds of pages of flashbacks, in some cases there would be 20 different subjects on one page. We had something about sharks, something about weather, something about mood, and something about rescue. So I ended up color coding and time coding everything to try to place it in the framework of this 17 hours in the water. I had different color pens. Some things dealing with personal reflections I marked in one color, important statistics I marked in another. Then we went through and tried to assign a time marker to each subject. After I got the lead, I went through these notes — spread all over a hotel room, on dressers and beds — and found everything that dealt with the first hours. I needed this system to give me some semblance of order.

Doesn't the structure of your story bring the reader through an emotional cycle of despair/ hope/greater despair/greater hope?

I thought about that a lot. And at one point, I asked myself whether I was stringing out this story to the point where the reader would just like to scream "My God! Will she finally tell us what happened?" But really, that's very much like life is. I felt that other people experience the same sorts of ups and downs. It just seemed very true to life to me.

Along with the brilliant quotations from Hal, you include some amazing anecdotes, such as the sharks nibbling on his legs.

We were sitting in the living room and it was one of the first times Hal felt that he could talk about the story. It was the day he got out of the hospital. He was feeling so bad once he got into that house and started thinking about Dianne. We were looking at his legs because he had all these shark bites on his legs. He was telling us how he felt the shark nibbling at his foot. And he said "Give me your hand, Mary Ellen," and I put out my hand, and he used his fingers like jaws and he said "First he took a hold here, and then he moved up here." And I just wanted to scream. It was such a dramatic thing. My reaction was "My God! if this were a movie, it would have such impact. How will I tell this to the readers so they'll have some visual idea of what happened."

Did the story change much through editing process?

I went back to a simple formula that I depended on in news stories and that was "Am I answering every possible question a reader is going to have." It was Phil Reed who came up with the sentence: "Not a single lifejacket, seat cushion or fragment of wreckage remained afloat." That was something we had missed. He said it was very important to stress that. One of the funniest things: I had used the line "The ambulance whisked Hal to the hospital." Phil read that and said "Hell! All ambulances whisk. I've never seen an ambulance that didn't whisk. It's goddam trite. Get it out of there." I was really amused because I thought: Here I've got this tremendous story, and I've been able to do all these good things, and then I use a work like *whisk*. It made me realize how important it was to have good editors.

Did Hal read the story?

He was absolutely overwhelmed. It was like reliving it for him. I sent him a copy before we went to press because there were so many technical things, about air speed and distance, that I felt he had to go over it. His reaction was that it seemed like I had been there.

Any reaction from readers?

All the letters were beautiful. They all responded greatly to the spiritual aspect. People said that it gave them the courage to go on and face their problems. One woman said it changed her life.

EDITOR'S NOTE: Thomas Oliphant, 33, came to the Boston Globe out of Harvard College and began covering economics, urban affairs and the anti-war movement in the early 1970s. In 1971 he was assigned to Washington and in the same year obtained the Pentagon Papers for The Globe. In 1974 he joined the editing desk that directed The Globe's Pulitzer Prize winning coverage of school desegregation in Boston. Oliphant returned to Washington in 1976. When the Great Blizzard crushed New England on February 6, 1978, Oliphant made his way from Washington to Boston where he helped write and edit a smashing 24-page special section on the storm. The section included 64 photos and involved the work of 20 reporters. Five stories from that section, reprinted here, were recognized by ASNE for their writing excellence.

The Boston Globe has a daily circulation of more than 400,000 and a Sunday circulation of more than 670,000.

1979
Prize Winner
News/Non-Deadline

Thomas Oliphant

FEBRUARY 19, 1978

It was 5 a.m., Sunday, February 5, 1978. The teletype machine in the headquarters of the Massachusetts State Police on Commonwealth avenue in Boston stuttered, then sprang to life.

The message originated in the National Weather Service office at Logan Airport.

"Snow is expected to spread into the state tonight and continue on Monday . . . Increasing northeasterly winds tonight and on Monday may cause considerable blowing and drifting . . . A substantial snowfall may come from it."

Francis Rexroad, the meteorologist who had the message sent to the state police and a host of other private and public agencies who use the service, didn't stop there.

He and his two coworkers on that shift made special phone calls to some of the key ones.

Something was brewing, they said, something big. You better get ready.

Just how bad that "something" would be, however, no one could know that sunny, quiet Sunday in February.

Not Francis Rexroad, not Sister Eileen O'Leary of St. Bartholemew's Parish in Needham, not Michael S. Dukakis of Brookline, not Mrs. Claire Young from Canton, not Dan McWilliams in his Winthrop home, and not Mrs. Madelyn Burdick in her home in the Beachmont section of Revere.

They could not possibly know that within 48 hours something would happen that would forever alter their lives — and in the case of Mrs. Young and 28 other people in Massachusetts, end them.

What was coming was an assault by nature that would wreck whole sections of coastal communities, strand thousands of people on roads under the most harrowing of conditions, cause hundreds of millions of dollars of damage.

It would bring out the very best in many people and the worst in some, it would disrupt the routines of life for everyone, bring people and neighborhoods together in shared misfortune, forge the first genuine personal bonds between a governor and the citizenry, and, for all who lived through it, leave memories that would last forever.

It began days before, with an extraordinary interaction of the air, the sea, the earth, the sun and the moon. These all seemed to conspire to make the Great Blizzard of '78 as bad as it could possibly be.

Across the North American continent, air generally moves in soft, waving bands from west to east.

But on Saturday, those bands buckled over the East Coast and turned north toward Canada, collecting, as they arrived, the dry, cold Arctic air that tends to sit there during the winter.

Then, the layers of air buckled again and headed south, where trouble also just happened to be brewing.

All week, weather watchers had noticed the air pressure dropping in spots off the Carolina coast. Sooner or later, when that happens, a storm forms.

What happens, and did in this case, is that the low pressure area sucks in the surrounding air currents and blows them straight up and out of the mass with great intensity, where they begin to circulate counter-clockwise.

This motion produces energy, enough energy for the system to move north.

But none of this had occurred when Francis Rexroad had that message sent out on Sunday morning. He merely saw the probability of it happening.

It wasn't until Sunday night and early Monday morning that Rexroad's worst fears began to materialize.

Force A (the warm air storm) met Force B (the cold air mass). More energy, more movement, more wind.

All day Sunday, the messages from the weather service had grown progressively more serious. Then, at ten o'clock Monday morning they became openly ominous.

"Eight to sixteen inches expected in most sections. The snow will be accompanied by strong easterly winds resulting in considerable blowing and drifting . . . Extensive flooding of low-lying coastal areas is expected at time of high tides both tonight and Tuesday morning . . . Traveling will become very hazardous later today and should be curtailed except in emergency."

That message got to the official clients of the weather service. It did not get to Dan McWilliams, or Claire Young or Madelyn Burdick.

For all they knew, what was happening Monday morning was just another snow storm, with a lot of wind.

After all, hadn't they just come through a storm barely two weeks before, which had dumped a record 21.6 inches of snow on the Boston area?

They had no way of knowing that this would not be "just another snow storm" — that unusual atmospheric conditions would cause it to become the most devastating blizzard of the century.

By a tragic coincidence, the huge storm was to become stalled over Massachusetts just as it reached peak intensity, trapped by a ridge of cold, heavy polar air to the north.

And as it did, the winds and the sea were to converge in a combined assault that was to wreak havoc on Massachusetts' coastline. With the high tide due at 10 p.m. Monday, and the sea already whipped to a frenzy by intensifying winds, it just so happened there was a full moon.

The earth, the sun and the moon had moved into relative positions creating their strongest possible pull on the tides.

To the people of Massachusetts, this meteorological monster only became visible as its Sunday punch hit them squarely on the jaw Monday afternoon and evening.

Exposed and helpless, there was only time to try to roll with it and, in thousands of cases, to try to stay alive.

Massachusetts' longest night had begun.

The scene was eerie, and the man was worried.

The parking lot was snow-laden. The winds howled. The seas slammed against the building on the wharf.

But inside Anthony's Pier 4, the main dining room was empty, quiet.

Upstairs, in his second-floor office-apartment, Anthony Athanas, one of those whose name means Boston, was alone.

He wasn't worried about his restaurant. He was worried about the *Peter Stuyvesant*, his floating palace. In the savage seas, the old Hudson River boat had moved about six inches in its elaborate cradle, and Athanas was worried because that had never happened before.

It was nearly midnight, Monday night.

For a decade, the *Peter Stuyvesant* had, after her retirement as a cruise ship in New York, served as the site of hundreds of political affairs, business dinners and other functions.

For Athanas, she was his special, prized possession.

Everywhere he traveled, he would pick up something special to add to the *Stuyvesant's* lavish appointments.

And he had gone to complex and costly lengths to make the vessel secure.

She rested on a specially-designed wooden grid. Attached to the front and rear were two big pieces of steel.

And into them ran two long pipes, each 70 feet long and 16 inches in diameter. The pipes, in turn, were anchored to the parking lot on the dock; they had been hammered into bedrock and encased in 40-ton concrete blocks.

But on Monday night, as the full fury of the hurricane force winds pounded at the ship, the iron and concrete mooring began to seem as fragile as Scotch tape.

Athanas called the Coast Guard and a Boston tow boat company. Could some craft be spared to come up next to the *Peter Stuyvesant* to help stabilize her? he asked.

The answer was no. All boats were only for use in life-or-death situations.

Athanas looked at his watch. It was a little after 1 a.m. He looked at his ship; she had moved some more, but there was nothing to be done.

Two hours later, Athanas smelled something funny, acrid. For the first time he worried about his safety. It didn't smell like a fire, but he decided to check downstairs anyway.

As he stood up, he felt like he was on a movie stage. The lights in his office suddenly burned super-bright as a power surge raced through the building.

Glancing out the window, he saw the power lines to the *Peter Stuyvesant* snap, shooting sparks that suddenly illuminated the adjacent parking lot.

Now Athanas was running down the stairs. As he reached the main dining room, the source of the smell was obvious.

The power surge had overtaxed the fluorescent lights and they had burned out. In the flickering, dim glow of the wall lights, Athanas looked around and saw a hair-raising sight: his electric cash registers were smoking.

That was when Athanas looked out the window again at the *Peter Stuyvesant*.

She was gone.

The *Peter Stuyvesant* had toppled out of her cradle into the sea. The sound of the final wrenching must have been deafening, but all Athanas heard was the northeast wind.

□

The ship is insured and possibly salvageable, but, to Athanas, irreplaceable.

"No matter how much they give me," he said later, "I don't know if it's salvageable. I can't restore it the same way. The shopping in London, throughout the East in antique shops, anywhere I was I'd always be looking for something for the boat. I can't do it the same way again."

The *Peter Stuyvesant* was a landmark for a decade, but it was the sea that left its mark on her.

The terror of the storm prevailed well into Tuesday night for much of southern New England. If its tenor changed as day turned to night, with easing winds and an end to the snow, its danger remained.

For the coast, there was the threat of the third high tide since the blizzard began. It would again hurl rocks and sand and water, smashing windows and then walls with its force.

Along miles of Massachusetts coastline Tuesday, hundreds of people were suddenly destitute, the raging waters robbing them even of their cars, their means of escaping the piles of rubble that once were their homes.

And along the miles of highways Tuesday, thousands of people were also immobilized, stranded in their cars under mounds of

snow, stranded far from their homes, in their cars but unable to use them to get back.

The problem was brutally simple. The state's roadway system had virtually shut down.

Motorists on the clogged highways couldn't get out. Fire trucks responding to alarms couldn't get through the unplowed streets to fires burning out of control. Ambulances couldn't reach the ill and the elderly. And on Rte. 128, until every vehicle was checked, no one knew how many commuters might be sick, dead or dying in their cars.

It would be days before even a semblance of order returned to the transportation system. And it will be months, even years, before recovery is completed for those whose homes and property had been laid to waste by the savagery of this winter storm.

At some point Tuesday, the people of Massachusetts knew that one problem was over — and another was just beginning.

The struggle back had started.

Along Rte. 128 and its feeder roads, the first people rescued were arriving at shelters before dawn. Their new homes were motels, factories, houses, golf clubs, Red Cross centers, town halls, restaurants, armories, stores, police stations — and in Needham, the convent, church and school of St. Bartholomew's Parish.

Sister Eileen O'Leary woke up at 4 a.m. The convent was filling up with people, anxious to call home to tell their people they were alive. They were very tense, hyper, she thought. Many were shivering, even though it was warm in the suddenly crowded convent. They shivered for hours from the shock of the ordeal on the highway.

Needham firefighter Bob Wade arrived at the parish complex at 7 a.m. with a truck-load of sandwich makings and an air of command. Like so many New Englanders, super-market owner Bud Roche had come through. He told Wade, "Take what you need, those people are scared and cold and pretty soon they're going to be starved."

Two professional cooks volunteered to work, and Wade put them in charge of the kitchen. A few miles away at a photographic processing plant, 57 people were going to cook frozen pot pies in print driers before the day was out. But St. Bartholomew's had a cafeteria.

Wade surveyed the situation of which he suddenly was in charge: Medical problems had to be a top priority. He counted heart patients, cancer patients and pregnant women among his refugees. He wrote down what each needed, plowed his four-wheel drive truck through the snowy streets, got the medicine from the local hospital and arranged for the transfer of the people who most needed comfort to a seminary on Rte. 135.

The parishioners of St. Bartholomew's by this time were pitching in, hauling food, pillows, blankets — even magazines — to their church on sleds and toboggans, in backpacks on skis and snowshoes.

People helped people in need. All day. All night. Everywhere. Wade came up with what rescued engineer Jack Fargo called "the miracle of the tuna fish" — hundreds of cans of it, which volunteer cooks turned into a nourishing casserole for 1500 people by 4 p.m.

□

As the stranded motorists in Needham took their first spoonfuls of the warm casserole, Gerry Villani was nibbling on a bag of pretzels, the only food left in the pumping station on Revere's Broadsound avenue.

When they pulled him to safety a few hours earlier, his skin was a bright, lobster red, his hands and feet were numb. The three hours of standing atop his truck, waves lapping at his feet, had taken its toll.

Jack Whitnell, a 66-year-old Metropolitan District Commission tunnel inspector who'd thought about retiring in a few months, pulled the wet clothes from Villani and hung them in a back room to dry. He took off his own sweater and wrapped the driver's feet in it.

And then, Jack Whitnell did something no one expected. He pulled off his remaining shirt and hugged the short, stocky Villani, wrapping his arms around him. Whitnell hoped that his own body warmth would provide the gradual heat that Villani needed.

A few hours later, the men would be carried to safety at a Revere Beach restaurant where warm food and strong drink was waiting free of charge. They would begin the task of resuming their lives.

Up and down the coastline, there were clues that things were improving. The familiar white disaster trucks with red crosses on the doors could be seen shuttling back and forth through whatever streets were still passable. The olive jeeps of the Massachusetts National Guard drove quickly now through the snowdrifts.

And still the people streamed in to shelters. There were 1260 refugees counted at breakfast Wednesday morning at St. Bartholomew's.

The bright, clear sun bode well for the day ahead. Inside the Scituate High School gymnasium, the 600 temporary residents seemed to sprawl into every corner of the room, some sleeping, some worrying, a few talking quietly to each other. Babies cried, dogs barked and the great search began.

The sun brought a new sense of purpose to February's victims. Throughout the state, they began looking for someone or something — a husband, a wife, a place to stay, a supermarket that was open, a ride back home to see what was left, an electrician, a repairman, a priest, a doctor, a word of encouragement wherever it was offered.

□

Frank Paradiso climbed down from the attic in his house on Revere's Broadsound avenue and looked at the high-water marks four feet up on his first-floor walls. Without heat and electricity and with his wife and three children, he'd weathered the storm in the waterfront home. He'd be damned if he was going to leave now.

Gerry Villani was back behind the wheel of another snowplow. He'd be damned if nearly dying was going to make him miss a day of work.

Andy Burdick, assured that Madelyn was safe, was walking back to his house. He'd be damned if the family's next home was going to be anywhere near the ocean.

During the night, the small, cedar-shingled house had toppled off its cinder block and piling foundation, finally settling some eight feet from where it had once been. The back of the house was missing, hidden somewhere in the rubble at the end of the street 100 yards away. A broken main spewed water into the street. "This house is going right to the junkyard," he said.

At Boston's Logan Airport, specially-trained US Army snowfighters arrived with massive bulldozers and front-end loaders in C130s and C5As from Ft. Bragg, N.C. They headed for Rte. 128 to tackle millions of tons of snow.

The soldiers tore out guard rails on the median strip, had the steel cut off at ground level with torches and hauled cars from the clogged southbound side of the highway to the cleared northbound side.

More people got home, some walking, many miles. At St. Bartholomew's, Sister Eileen helped parishioners Paul and Dorothy Brooks draw up lists of people still to be transported. The National Guard trucks continued to rumble out of the complex around the clock. Travel by private vehicle was still prohibited.

Wednesday and Thursday saw beautiful dawns breaking over a region still paralyzed. Nature had handed New England its worst winter beating in a century, then turned around and bathed its handiwork in bitter irony. The problems remaining were catastrophic in the whole, staggering when considered one by one.

But for some, the end was finally in sight. On Friday, the last of the refugees, 60 truckers, left St. Bartholomew's. They had spent the week volunteering for every job imaginable, from filling in for town plow operators to helping to wash dishes to shoveling out townspeople.

Sister Eileen made them all "big, big sandwiches — truck driver sandwiches."

And because some of them were getting a bit "crummy" after so many days at the church complex, Sister Eileen arranged for them to take showers and then went over to the convent to get the hair dryer for them to use.

Saturday, the last of the vehicles on Rte. 128 was pulled free of the snow.

By Sunday, Jack Fargo and the thousands of other hostages of winter were home with their families.

St. Bartholomew's was back to its regular routine — although it isn't every Sunday that Cardinal Medeiros sends a personal note of thanks to a congregation.

And Bob Wade was putting his snowmobile in tip-top shape — not for a trip to New Hampshire, but "just in case there's more snow before this is cleaned up, because people's lives might depend on snow machines."

For others, with more to worry about than snowmobiles, it was a weekend filled with little jobs, of shoveling snow and ice from the basement, tearing out the water-soaked wall-to-wall carpeting. Work to do while waiting for Tuesday.

For the thousands of families in eastern Massachusetts who felt the brunt of the Blizzard of 1978, Tuesday would be the judgment day. Federal representatives would arrive at 13 relief centers around the state. They would know who was eligible for what and why.

By early morning, Revere's victims had lined up by the hundreds outside the door at St. Anthony's Church in Revere. They talked of low-interest loans, tax breaks and money for food and clothing. Money from Washington to help the little people of Revere.

Money for everything from eyeglasses to motel rooms. From shoes to food. From dentures to tranquilizers.

For some, it wasn't enough.

Dr. Barbara Burns, a psychologist at Boston's Lindemann Health Center, walked among Revere's disaster victims. She listened to them talk, comforted them when they cried, tried to help them deal with an unprecedented ordeal.

What had happened, she explained, could change their lives. There would be marital rifts, when a partner feared moving back near the sea. There would be indecision about what to do. There would be feelings that they, and they alone, were jinxed. There would be problems getting along in cramped hotel rooms. There would be fears of selling their house to someone else, afraid that the purchaser might someday drown. Would it be their fault?

"We try to get them focusing on reality," explained Dr. Burns. "To look at what they got out with. Their lives.

"We tell them to do something that will make them comfortable. And we tell them to do it now while they can come to terms with it.

"This storm will be a part of their lives forever."

The governor with the black, wavy hair, wearing a turtleneck sweater as he spoke on the television to the people . . .

The tanned mayor of Boston, stuck on vacation in Palm Beach.

Comr. Joe Jordan of the Boston Police Dept., trying to catnap on the floor in the operations room at headquarters and nearly getting trampled by a lieutenant . . .

Presidential aides Stuart Eizenstat and Jack Watson ducking in and out of the Oval Office, telling Jimmy Carter what Mother Nature was doing to Massachusetts . . .

Joe D. Winkle from the Federal Disaster Assistance Administration, closing up his work after a flood in Asheville, N.C., to head for Boston to coordinate the response to the 79th disaster of his career . . .

House Speaker Thomas P. O'Neill Jr. lobbying presidential aide Jody Powell . . .

The acting mayor of Boston in the mayor's absence, City council President Lawrence DiCara, holding onto parking meters for dear life as he stumbled through the wind and snow in the predawn hours of Tuesday, February 7 . . . These were some of the scenes of government in crisis.

At all levels, from town halls to the White House, the handling of the natural disaster that struck Massachusetts of Feb. 6 was spiced by petty politics, posturing, spurious claims of influence and elbowing for the limelight. It is always thus.

That is because the stakes for the people are so high.

When disaster strikes, it is to government that people are forced by circumstance to turn: For information, for instructions, for the cleanup, and above all for the aid that is the principal stimulus for the rebuilding process.

Throughout a wild week, the citizens of Massachusetts caught some revealing glimpses of three men in particular, as they observed them through the uniquely sharp lens of personal privations: Michael Dukakis, Jimmy Carter, and Kevin White.

The governor from Brookline — painted for so long as a cold, aloof, uncaring figure — would forge the first genuine, personal bond between himself and his constituents since taking over the corner office in 1975. And he would do it through that most impersonal of mediums, television. He would also take charge, initially in something of a vacuum.

The President from rural Georgia would again show himself to be a special friend of the Yankee state that gave him his largest majority in the 1976 election, and whose best-known congressman, Speaker Thomas P. O'Neill Jr., is Carter's closest legislative ally.

But the President would also show there are limits to his largesse.

The mayor from Boston would, in the main, defer to others. Fuming in private over the political misfortune of his vacation timing, he was savvy enough to know that the problem was larger than his city. He resolved not to be an obstacle to the efforts made beyond its boundaries to deal with it.

To subordinates, White delegated the task of keeping the nose of city government to the grindstone of essential services: Public safety, clearing streets and getting life's necessities to the isolated, the old and the poor.

But even beyond that, government ceased for a while to be a dirty word. Leaving aside those with official titles, this was, above all, the case at the level where services actually get delivered: The MDC cop, the National

Guardsman, the public works employee. These and others like them were the ones who made the system work.

□

Monday, Feb. 6.

On Beacon Hill, Michael Dukakis sat with his closest staff members. The heavy snow was already falling and he had sent state workers home early. There was only one real question they were discussing: Whether to run the government the next day with a skeleton crew.

In Washington, Jimmy Carter spent his most important moments that afternoon huddled for the fourth day with Egyptian President Anwar Sadat.

In Palm Beach, Kevin White was with his wife. The weather, he said later, was "awful, just lousy there, too. Katherine and I froze, I had no vacation, didn't even swim in the pool . . ."

For a change, the politicians were in the same boat with the people. They were equally unaware of, and unprepared for, the tests nature would put them to in just a matter of hours.

☐

Gov. Michael Dukakis began to take command of a shaken state between 8 and 10 p.m. that Monday night in the improbable setting of David Brudnoy's talk show at the WHDH studio on Stuart street — a monthly stop for the man who was doing "town meeting" long before anyone heard of Jimmy Carter.

In between questions, he took calls from his chief secretary, David Liederman, who relayed to him two important requests. One came from Comr. John Snedeker of the Metropolitan District Commission, asking that he urge residents of the low-lying sections of Winthrop to evacuate their homes before high tide.

The other came from state Civil Defense headquarters in Framingham, where director Robert Cunningham wanted him to declare a state of emergency.

Dukakis did both, on the air.

And he also called out the National Guard.

Judging from many of the show's callers, it was difficult to know that the worst blizzard of the century was occurring.

Right after he pleaded with residents of Winthrop Shore drive to evacuate at once, he took a call from a woman who complained about the state's 10 percent tax on unearned income.

☐

The next morning, driven to MDC headquarters in a truck with a scoop shovel attached, the governor met with Liederman, Snedeker, MDC official Michael Goldman and another aide, Lou Murray.

It was on this occasion, beginning about eight, that the decision was made that may, in the end, prove the most memorable. The governor banned private driving with almost no exceptions.

The way had already been paved for such a step. Nearly three hours earlier, after getting a full report on the previous night's devastation. Liederman had begun calling radio and television stations with the message that people should stay in their homes.

At that meeting, the decision was virtually automatic. There were no arguments; it was clear to all that this was the only way to give street plows a fighting chance against the mountains of snow.

Nor was there any serious attempt at prior consultation with city and town officials. Instead, the governor and his aides consulted a statute book for their legal support.

Later that morning, Dukakis also asked that arrangements be made for him to go on all area TV stations through the pooled facilities of nearby Channel 7.

He would appear on television three more times that day, and at least once a day thereafter until the end of the weekend.

Usually he spoke with just a few notes, but occasionally he ad libbed — in clear, concise syntax. He imparted the day's vital information, issued orders and advice; in short he was in complete command.

It worked beyond what anyone had imagined, so well in fact that one of the better bits of trivia from the storm Monday was the buried impact of an announcement by Middlesex County Sheriff John Buckley that he would seek the Republican nomination for governor this fall.

☐

Jimmy Carter's Washington awoke Tuesday morning with a little of New England's snow on the ground and a big request in the air. In the middle of the night Rhode Island Gov. J. Joseph Garrahy had phoned the new head of the Federal Disaster Assistance Administration, William Wilcox.

With his state buried in snow, Garrahy wanted a declaration of emergency by the President so troops and heavy equipment could be dispatched to assist in locating the pavement on Rhode Island's roads.

When Wilcox got to the office that morning, he called Dukakis' office and asked if Massachusetts would be putting an application in the hopper as well. It would, he was told.

Liederman called Carter aide Jack Watson later that morning to let him know one was on the way, and Watson alerted the President's office.

Carter made it official for Rhode Island at 3:45 p.m., and for Massachusetts, and also-stricken Connecticut, at 5:47.

It was an important development in the process of securing aid, but no sooner had word seeped from the White House to Capitol Hill of the President's action than the time-honored race was on — who could leak it to the press first and claim some credit.

The race was won by none other than Kevin White, who had thought it wise to fly to Washington for the day rather than spend any more time in Florida as he awaited a means of getting back to Boston.

But the mayor blew it. In an interview on the six o'clock news by long-distance hookup

White mistakenly praised the President for declaring the state a "disaster area" when, in fact, Carter had declared a state of emergency. It was no small error, since in the federal lexicon, "disaster" means help in the form of men and equipment, and "emergency" means help in the form of cold, hard cash.

When Carter at least made the mayor an accidental prophet three days later by declaring eight coastal counties disaster areas, for real, the fight for credit was among the Bay State congressional offices.

An aide to Sen. Edward Kennedy made the first call to a reporter with the "news," while the senator himself, in another room, called radio stations in Boston.

A close second went to Milton's Rep. James A. Burke, with third place to Boston's Rep. Joe Moakley.

What none of them knew was that first prize for impact went to the state's news anchorman of the week — Michael Dukakis —who announced the Carter decision at his daily televised news conference.

□

Back in Boston late Tuesday afternoon, there were some anxious moments at Joe Jordan's police department. An outbreak of looting had occurred in Dorchester's Codman Square, mostly at a food store, but spilling into the struggling business district.

And there were other — though less serious — incidents in South Boston, Charlestown and along Center Street in West Roxbury.

To make matters worse, much of the city and nearly all the police stations were plunged into darkness by a fire at an electric company relay station.

From his experience in the ugly desegregation process three years ago, Jordan was well aware of how a city or a neighborhood can lose control of itself. He was worried.

It is still not precisely clear why the trouble suddenly died down the next day.

But the following must have had something to do with it: An ominous message was broadcast over the Boston media late Tuesday ordering all off-duty officers to report in full riot gear; the 100-odd people arrested for looting were held in stunningly high bails; and the snow was not exactly a fast track.

☐

By Thursday morning, there was some heat being felt in the governor's office, and it wasn't all from the antiquated old radiators.

It was from certain large businesses that wanted to reopen.

It was from some suburbs that wanted the driving ban eased.

And it was even from Dukakis himself, who felt road conditions were improving and that any means of relaxing the daily burdens of his snowbound citizens should be explored.

So that day, the governor was thinking of relaxing the ban enough to permit perhaps a work day through mass transit like the one that eventually occurred the following Monday.

In fact, he was planning to.

But MBTA official Ken Campbell heard about it, and when he saw Dukakis aide Michael Widmer at the MDC command post that afternoon, he told him it wouldn't work. There was too much equipment still unrestored to service, he said. If the governor went ahead, there would be chaos.

Widmer got on the phone with Dukakis, and that was that.

The governor was also getting reports that some communities where relaxation of the ban had occurred without authorization were experiencing traffic jams that were getting in the way of the snow clean up.

One town, Framingham, asked outright for permission to end the ban. The state Civil Defense people said to go ahead and see what happened.

What happened was chaos. In two hours, town officials were clamoring to Liederman for reinstatement. He obliged.

The experience was illustrative. As the governor's point man, Liederman regularly saw how thankful communities were that a tough decision had been taken off their hands.

It was on Wednesday that the governor embarked on perhaps his most critical project — cutting a deal with Jimmy Carter to get as much of the state as possible declared a disaster area.

Dukakis' man in the effort was the lieutenant governor, Thomas P. O'Neill 3d. Carter's representative was White House aide Greg Schneiders. Beginning Wednesday, Schneiders told O'Neill that a state applicant — restricted to the flood and wind damage to coastal counties — would be quickly approved.

But the governor's staff was stalling, advising Dukakis to try as well for all the blizzard-impacted counties, including Middlesex and Worcester, and let the White House take the rap for turning them down.

At first, five counties were acceptable to the White House: Essex, Suffolk, Norfolk, Plymouth, and Bristol. A telegram requesting a disaster designation for them was sent to the White House Friday morning.

Rep. Gerry Studds had heard about all this and he was livid because it did not include three flood-damaged counties in his district: Dukes, Barnstable and Nantucket. Also on Friday, after Studds was told that those counties would also be acceptable, a second telegram was sent to the White House.

At four that afternoon, the President declared a "major disaster in the state of Massachusetts as a result of coastal flooding."

But the Massachusetts people kept trying for more. O'Neill kept pressing for the inclusion of Worcester and Middlesex counties and an extension of the declaration in the others to include damage from ice and snow.

But Schneiders held firm on adding any more counties. The White House was afraid of the very costly precedent that would be set by making disasters out of snowstorms.

Nonetheless, the White House tried to soften the blow. On the one hand, Carter decided on Tuesday, Feb. 14, to extend the terms of the disaster proclamation to include snow and ice damage on the grounds that it was impossible to distinguish what force of nature had caused the damage in coastal areas.

In addition, a little ruse was concocted. On that same Tuesday, the federal disaster agency "announced" that Worcester and Middlesex counties would be eligible for special Small Business Administration loans. In fact, they are automatically eligible for them under law as areas directly adjacent to a disaster area.

Still, the bottom line is that Massachusetts did unusually well in Washington. The states of New Hampshire and Rhode Island have also filed requests for disaster area status.

To date, they haven't heard a word.

He named his pilot boat *Can Do*, and when no one else dared challenge a wild sea, Frank Quirk would say, "I've got to give it my best shot."

Gloucester had awarded him two Mariner's Medals for heroism during rescues, defying the sea with his courage, his seamanship and his custom-made boat. On the night of Feb. 6, he set out from Gloucester in the middle of what was to become New England's worst storm of this century, hoping to reach an oil tanker aground in Salem Sound.

It was the last voyage of Frank Quirk's life.

For the seamen of Gloucester, stormy weather means listening to marine radios. After lunch at the Cape Ann Marina Lounge, Quirk headed for The High Performance Marina where the *Can Do* was docked to listen to the radios and put the finishing touches on a boat that was always shipshape and spotless.

Late in the afternoon, his friends Dave Warner, Kenny Fuller, Dave Curley, Charlie Bucko and young Mark Galinas came aboard.

Shortly after 6 p.m., the six heard the Greek-registered tanker *Global Hope* radio the Coast Guard station at Gloucester. The message was difficult to hear, but the ship apparently was taking on water in the engine room and its captain believed the hull was split.

At 6:12 p.m. the Coast Guard dispatched three vessels to aid *Global Hope*, a 44-foot rescue boat from the Gloucester station, the 210-foot cutter *Decisive* from waters off Cape Cod and the 95-foot patrol boat *Cape George*.

Quirk decided to help. He called the Coast Guard and told him his plan. The Coast Guard called back and told him not to, that the seas were too rough.

But as Quirk told his friend Keith Trefy, the Gloucester harbor master, "I've got to give it my best shot."

The *Can Do* was under way at 7:36 p.m. by Mark Galinas' watch. The 16-year-old Gloucester High School student was ashore. The last time he had gone out with Capt. Quirk he missed a couple of days of school, and he couldn't do it again.

He had given Bucko his new coat.

Shortly after the *Can Do* set out, the Coast Guard station asked Quirk to keep a lookout for its 44-footer, which had grounded.

The wind was blowing between 40 and 70 knots, the seas were running 15 to 20 feet, and visibility was 50 yards at best in blinding snow.

The sea smashed Quirk's boat, taking first the *Can Do's* radar, compass and fathometer. Then it took the power and some of Quirk's blood when an enormous wave shattered the pilot house window where he stood.

Then, the implacable sea took Quirk and

the four men who had accompanied him on his last mission.

Much of the rest of the story can be told in Frank Quirk's own words, and finally in his silence.

On the night the *Can Do* was lost at sea with five aboard, amateur radio ham operator Mel Cole of Beverly was in contact with Capt. Frank Quirk and several unidentified members of the crew. Following are the last messages received from the ship:

(At 10 p.m. the *Can Do* advised the Coast Guard she would return to Gloucester after a large wave from astern had broken the AM antenna, making the radar inoperative. The Coast Guard later advised the *Can Do* that high seas prevented an escort mission.)

10:30 p.m. — Quirk: "Really wild out here. Not sure of position."

12 a.m. — *Can Do*: "Still cannot see Gloucester Harbor entrance."

1 — Unidentified *Can Do* crew member: "This is not a drill. This is not a drill. May Day. May Day."

1:20 — Unidentified crew member: "We may have hit the breakwater."

1:35 — *Can Do* crew member to Gloucester station: "Lost pilot house window, our radar out. Our position unknown. Action extremely violent."

1:45 — Quirk: "They've patched me up and we're holding our own for now."

1:55 — *Can Do* crew member shouted: "We've had it."

(At 2:00 a.m. Coast Guard Boston mistakenly advised all stations that the *Can Do* crew was ashore and safe in Magnolia.)

2:10 — Quirk: "We've got an anchor set and we're holding our own, taking a beating but am trying to build up some power and get things started again."

2:15 — Quirk: "Well, no luck on power. Thirty-two volt batteries all shorted out. I have a mattress stuffed in the window to keep the seas out and the boys have me pretty well patched up from cuts by flying glass. Water's not building in boat."

2:35 — Quirk to Cole: "Mel, getting pretty cold and weak here. Guess the loss of blood caused this. Keep getting wet, too."

2:45 — Cole to *Can Do*: "Frank, want to try your CB?"

Quirk: "We're pretty well wedged between the table, here. Don't think we'll move. Really rippen' out here. Last attempt on (Channel) three was no good."

3:30 — Quirk: "Beverly Base (Cole). The *Can Do*. We're getting pretty wet up here. Hatch is loose and we're gonna try to move aft."

Cole: "OK, Frank, take your time and try to get all the cover over you possible . . . Frank, it's only about two hours to dawn and latest weather promises abating seas. Gloucester Coast Guard will get a 44-footer going to your position then."

Quirk: "OK, Mel, we'll hold on. Sure wish I could raise some power. It's cold and really hoppin' out here but we're making it."

Cole: "OK, Frank, Don't waste your batteries. You were breaking up on that last transmission. Get some rest and I'll be here when you come back."

4:00 — Cole to *Can Do* — No answer.

4:30 — Cole to *Can Do* — No answer.

4:35 — Boston Coast Guard to Cole: "Are you still able to raise the *Can Do*?"

Cole: "That's a negative. It has been over an hour since my last contact. We'll keep trying."

(Cole remained on the air until 10 a.m. Tuesday trying futilely to make contact.)

NOTES AND COMMENTS

The tools of the writer's trade are many and varied. For an energetic reporter like Tom Oliphant, they include a faithful pair of sneakers, which he wears everywhere. They have become something of a trademark, invaluable for running after candidates in an election year. "When my boss Tom Winship (editor of *The Globe*) told me I had to go to a banquet to accept my ASNE writing award, I said 'Whadya think, boss? Should I rent a pair of shoes?' He thought about it for a half a second and said 'If you don't wear your sneakers, I'll kick your butt out of the dinner.'" So Tom Oliphant wore his sneakers. With a tuxedo.

A go-getter like Oliphant has little time to savor old stories, even when they are as brilliant as his narrative on the Blizzard of '78, a monster of a storm, and a grave test for any reporter, even one shod in Converse All-Stars.

Oliphant's stylish writing gave substance to *The Globe's* ambitious chronicle of the great storm and the people whose lives were changed by it. The narrative is so broad in scope that Oliphant wisely leads with an almost cosmic introduction, one that suggests the beginning of a James Michener novel: "It began days before, with an extraordinary interaction of the air, the sea, the earth, the sun and the moon." Oliphant begins at the beginning, in the atmosphere, tracing the meteorological forces that converged to crush New England. Before we see the storm through the eyes of the people, we see the people, through the eye of the storm.

People are the soul of Oliphant's account, united as they are in a democracy of hardship and grief: the nun, the politician, the homeowner, the motorist, the sea captain. As Oliphant says, "For a change, the politicians were in the same boat with the people. They were equally unaware of, and unprepared for, the tests nature would put them to in just a matter of hours."

By the time we move through the narrative, we have the feel of a whole people acting with "grace under pressure," behaving with kindness and civility, even when the trappings of civilization have been buried under tons of snow. It's the old New England story retold: the sanctity of hard work, the blessings wrought from ingenuity and stick-to-itiveness.

Oliphant's writing draws the reader through the long series for a number of reasons:

Visual description — Several scenes roll, in the mind's eye, like sequences from a Brian De Palma horror movie: "The power surge had overtaxed the fluorescent lights and they had burned out. In the flickering, dim glow of the wall lights, Athanas looked around and saw a hair-raising sight: his electric cash registers were smoking."

Startling anecdotes — "And then, Jack Whitnell did something no one expected. He pulled off his remaining shirt and hugged the short, stocky Villani, wrapping his arms around him. Whitnell hoped that his own body warmth would provide the gradual heat that Villani needed."

Coherent structure — In the first story, important characters are introduced without confusion. We meet them individually later in dramatic situations. New names and characters are gradually introduced and carefully developed, as in a good novel.

Writing about the human side of politicians — In government reporting, politicians are rarely developed as complex human characters. More often, they are treated like demi-gods, authority figures with larger than life strengths and weaknesses. Oliphant's political reporting here is especially astute. Not only do we see how the political process operates in a crisis, but the human side of government officials is revealed again and again through quotation and anecdote.

A sense of the dramatic — In the story about the death of Captain Quirk, no amount of florid description could be as sad or as dramatic as the final chronicling of the sparse, last messages from the helpless vessel.

In a live interview in Boston, editor Timothy Leland discussed the conception and execution of *The Globe's* Blizzard project. Later from Washington, Tom Oliphant, who assured us he was wearing sneakers, talked about his writing in a telephone conversation.

Interview with Roy Clark and Tim Leland

CLARK: Why did you decide to create a special section with these kinds of stories after the storm?

LELAND: We had a horrendous environmental story that affected everybody in the state, and we wanted a series of stories that would capture it. We sent out 20 reporters, and Tom Oliphant digested and assimilated their reports. This was more typical of a national magazine approach than a newspaper approach. His job was to be the premium writer, to take reports, tailor them and work out the structure in a complete way.

Why not just compile a series of factual reports?

Here we had this enormous event. We had committed ourselves to produce a special section. We didn't want to give the reader just a series of factual reports: how many people were stuck in their cars, how many inches of snow fell, how cold it was, how many people had to be fed. We wanted to present a mosaic, a picture of the event, the drama, a documentary film in print of an event of critical importance to everybody it touched.

How were you going to accomplish that?

Through people. We were going to capture the drama and the human terror of those few days. What it was like to be stranded in your car, or have water coming through your living room window. What was the sound of the snow, the sight of the blackness, the feel of the cold water coming through the streets. Our strategy was to tell the story through the eyes and in the words of the people who lived it. Each story begins with dramatic color. Each attempts to set a scene and put the reader inside it, to get the reader involved. Tom Oliphant is a stylist. He takes great interest in the way words appear on the page and the effect they have on readers.

The series is so ambitious that it must have been difficult to organize.

This whole thing has a structure, a drama. We tried not to introduce people and leave them in a moment of crisis without ever resolving it. You've got to build and construct each one as a small short story. Any novelist who brings in people gratuitously or any movie that doesn't take a theme and carry it through will be subject to severe criticism. You've got to build threads through any drama, whether it is a movie or a book or in this case a narrative. Editing a piece like this is like being an orchestra leader, making sure the woodwinds are in harmony with the brass and the brass is in the same rhythm as the percussions.

Interview with Thomas Oliphant

What was the most difficult problem you faced in writing and organizing these stories?

OLIPHANT: The staff had already spent two or three days just trying to cover this cataclysmic event for a daily paper. And then, all of a sudden, you have to tell the story in a grand fashion. And, of course, what you're missing is a fresh staff. That's one reason they asked me to help. I'm in the Washington bureau. I didn't arrive in Boston until Thursday morning and the blizzard hit Monday night.

Did coming into the story late help give you an overview of the crisis?

It did provide an interesting perspective. The airport remained closed for an entire week. So I had to take a night train to get there. And I recall as day was breaking and the train was coming into Massachusetts the sudden awesome sight of all this snow. It was almost more of a shock to me than to somebody who had seen it gradually accumulate. So in a sense *The Globe* got not only a fresh writer, but a fresh perspective.

As a reader, I derived several themes from the stories. One is the "democracy of suffering," that the snow and the misery fall on the rich and the poor, the weak and the powerful alike.

That simply grew out of the reporting. I think that came through our insistence that we would concentrate on what was happening to real people. So in effect by reporting the stories of people everywhere, that theme comes through. It reflects the reporting technique.

Another theme is the ability of people to act in civilized ways, even when the trappings of civilization are missing.

Again the reasoning was inductive, not deductive. Particularly in my case since I hadn't experienced the storm. So I was uniquely dependent on the raw material. I was able to go out and spend a couple of days in the aftermath of the blizzard which helped me a great deal. You've noticed a theme that we noticed, but it came out of the reporting and was not determined ahead of time.

How did you decide what kind of style to use?

The one thing I wanted was to write a narrative. My original conception was much more ambitious than what we were able to do. I would have wished that it could have been one great narrative from beginning to end. But because we only had five days to do it, there was no way to avoid breaking it up.

Why do you like the narrative style?

I think it's the best way to reconstruct major events. That's really the genre we're talking about here. Nothing beats narrative. And newspapers don't do enough of it.

Some of the visual scenes are very exciting, like the sight of the smoking electric cash registers. Is that something you work on?

It's something that all of us paid particular attention to. I was constantly saying to people: What did it look like? Describe it to me. Just think of what's involved here. Here is this great big old tub that's been converted into a floating bar and restaurant. The thing gets yanked off its moorings and tipped over in the middle of a furious blizzard. Well, if that's all you've said, you haven't said anything. The only way you can go is to pretend that you were standing there on the dock at Pier 4 and over the period of a couple of hours watched the forces gather that made it happen. It couldn't have been done but for the fact that the owner of the restaurant happened to be in his own place on land nearby. He was our eyes.

I was impressed with how even the politicians come across as real human characters rather than authority figures in this series.

Remember we're dealing with a cataclysmic news event, as awesome and as impressive to governors as it was to reporters and as it was to people whose lives were affected. Politicians don't take on the aura that they sometimes do when you're not talking about the normal course of events. The thing that I discovered in doing the reporting, whether it was talking to Senator Kennedy or the governor or the mayor — was that they all had the urge to tell the personal story. Just like talking to the guy who slept in his car on Route 128. It almost came pouring out of people. It was some of the easiest reporting on the governmental level that I've ever done. The urge to confess and tell all was strong.

In the beginning, you discuss the meteorological forces that led to the blizzard. This was done clearly and with some drama, even though I don't know a cold front from a high pressure area. I found myself very involved in this weather information.

The key to my being able to write that lead is that I didn't know anything about the weather either. I had no idea what produces wind, I don't know why the sky is blue, or any of that. I can remember talking to a stringer, a kid I was sending to the weather bureau, and I said "You go and ask everything. Do not let them use one word you don't understand, that you can't put into plain English for me." I wanted to take that storm from wherever the hell in the universe it originated and bring it to Boston. The thing I had going for me there was ignorance.

Do you think about readers much when you're writing?

Not as such. I'm one of these people who write primarily for themselves. I'm by far my sternest critic and biggest goad. The thing in my style I pay most attention to is not so much how things read, but how they sound. My crutches are alliteration, adjectives and adverbs, a consciousness of sound, the way words sound. To me writing is not merely read. There's something else that goes on when you're reading carefully that involves the sounds of those words. If someone was doing a scouting report on me, they'd probably pick that out as a character of my style.

Do you rewrite much?

Sometimes there isn't any time. In the case of this section, the actual writing was done in a 36-hour period. And you're talking about a good 50,000 words. When I have the time to recast things, I try to eliminate wordiness. In my case rewriting makes my stuff tighter. I tend to be a little bit too discursive. It's a distillation process more than an editing process. I have a tendency to say things in several sentences that really can be said better in one. *Distill* is my favorite verb to explain it.

EDITOR'S NOTE: *Everett S. Allen is 63 years old. He joined the staff of the New Bedford (Mass.) Standard-Times in 1938 after graduating from Middlebury (Vermont) College with a degree in English. For 41 years he has worked in New Bedford as a reporter, editor and editorial writer. He is the author of six books, including* This Quiet Place, a Cape Cod Chronicle, *published by Little, Brown, 1971. He has received many awards for his writing. But it took Allen ten years to convince his editors that there was room in the paper for his personal essays. His Sunday column, "The Present Tense," has run since January, 1966. He is about to retire as editorial page editor, but will continue his column and will work with young writers for the Ottaway Newspaper group. He is planning another book, this one dealing with the history of southern New England.*

The New Bedford Standard-Times is a member of the Ottaway Newspaper group. It has a daily circulation of more than 48,000 and a Sunday circulation of more than 50,000.

1979
Grand Prize Winner
Commentary

Everett S. Allen

FEBRUARY 12, 1978

Long ago, I conceived and developed what I have come to call an attitude of "frozen alertness," designed to get me through situations in which I want to appear to be listening without actually having to.

This came about because I was once forced to take a course in economics. I listened to the professor for the first half-hour of the first class in September, concluded that he might as well have been speaking Eskimo, which perhaps he was, and went back to the dormitory determined to invent a facial expression that would simulate rapt attention.

I practiced before the bathroom mirror some little time and finally was satisfied; obviously, there must be no glazing of the eyes, no wandering, no drowsy lowering of the lids, but rather a flattering, unfading eagerness, mouth slightly curled, ready to respond to the least attempt at humor.

It worked well. Although I sat in the front row of the classroom, and never heard another word that the professor said for the remainder of the year — being totally absorbed with thoughts about other things — as far as I know, he was unaware of my inattention. Once, the end-of-class bell rang and I was so preoccupied with wondering how whales can make themselves sink that I did not bolt from the classroom as everyone else did, but I like to think he put this down to exceptional interest in his lecture.

In any event, the other day at lunch, a young father sat next to me and launched into a monologue concerning his small child, who evidently does not eat well. This is not my favorite subject. Of my two children, one ate well and one did not, but now that they are grown and sensible, they both eat well and I could have saved myself the spasms of apoplexy that I devoted to the matter years ago.

I could have said this to the young father but this would not have been kind because what he really wanted was to fondle the subject, to examine it, to make a federal case of it, and to scrutinize every last carbohydrate. As with most people, when they get their teeth into their favorite subject, he did not really want a dialogue, either; he wanted to talk at me, not with me, about it. So I fixed my face into the attitude of "frozen alertness," munched my bacon, lettuce, and tomato sandwich and let my mind go wandering. "Let him enjoy himself," I thought paternally.

Because he had brought up the matter of diet and because there has always been brisk discussion as to whether young children who eat only one thing, day after day, are harming themselves or choosing wisely according to a basic instinct, I fell to thinking about Mr. MacGregor.

Mr. MacGregor lived alone in a little, neat house that was, as my grandmother would have said, "somewhat off to one side." He was not a large man, had a trim figure, wore his white hair clipped short, did odd jobs, went to bed early, and rose, so he said, at sunrise. He was not very talkative, but he was friendly, and from time to time, I would stop by his house, not so much for his company, I confess, but because the aroma therein was always great and always the same.

That, of course, was the clue to Mr. MacGregor's eccentricity; for all the years that I knew him, he ate only one thing, every day, and that was mince pie. I never asked him why; I do not know anyone who knew why — as opposed to our own age, when it is not only permissible, but virtually compulsory to ask anybody anything, those were years in which becoming reticence was commonly practiced.

It seemed to me a very personal matter. It may have been romanticizing on my part, but I chose to think perhaps he had been a victim of unrequited love and had thereupon sworn, in some lonely midnight pledge, that he would never again eat anything but mince pie. Do not, pray, ask me why he would do so; I do not pretend to know everything.

But the smells within his house — ah, me, for there were always mince pies under construction, cooling, baking, crisping, and all — the smells were such as to rebuild faith in man. Because the house was of no more than two or three rooms, there remained within it always the aura of his cooking, the uplifting, aromatic marriage of beef and Baldwins; of molasses, cider, and citron; of brandy, clove, and quinces; of nutmeg, pepper, and raisins, for he "built" his pies (the expression was his own) starting from the basic ingredients.

Although he would not have used the word, being embarrassed to do so, this one thing that he cooked, he cooked with love. I can remember now what it was like when it all began to come together in the wood-burning stove; the bubbling melding of parts, the daily miracle, the smelling of several things until finally it was the smelling of one magnificent thing only.

Anyway, on his 76th birthday, as a testimony to the soundness of his diet Mr. MacGregor announced that he would stand on his hands in his front yard. It was a spring morning and for the time of day and place, it drew a fair audience. There was a fellow just over the wall who was snaking out stumps, an elderly woman with a straw basket, two children bound for a brook to fish in, and a long-nosed collie. Sure enough, although the act was creaky, shaky, and brief, Mr. MacGregor stood on his hands. At which point, he fell in a heap on his back, with a yelp of pain. Events proved that nothing had happened to his back, but he had broken his ankle. I have no idea how he could have achieved that.

Later, I said to the doctor, "Do you think Mr. MacGregor's ankle broke because he eats only mince pies? Dietary deficiency? The doctor looked at me and replied, "Mr. MacGregor's ankle broke because he is 76 years old and was acting like a damned fool."

At about this point in my reverie, I became abruptly aware that the young father next to me had ended his discourse and was saying to me, "And what do you think of that?"

That, of course, is a nasty question if your mind has been far away. So, being still some-

what in the land of Mr. MacGregor, I replied
(since I supposed the young father at some
point must have consulted a pediatrician concerning the child's diet problem), "Well, I
think what the doctor said was absolutely
right."

The young father looked at me in the
strangest fashion, muttered something like
"um," rose, and departed. In retrospect, I concluded perhaps he had not mentioned anything about doctors and if not, I guess you
would have to say I missed that time.

Still, I have never maintained that "frozen
alertness" works without fail. It just works
often enough so that I have not given it up all
these years.

MARCH 26, 1978

There is the insistence of spring across the
marsh and beyond, even if the pools are still
cold and black and on the banks, the most
stubborn of last year's husks rattle in the
crisp westerly to remind of what was and is no
more.

("Israeli warplanes swooped into southern Lebanon today, aiming to knock out Palestinian artillery firing on Christian villages
in Israel's new security strip. The jet fighters
roared across Israel's northern border as the
guerrilla shells crashed around roads leading
to Marjayoun and Kleia, just beyond the
frontier.")

The new season is still little more than
an aura, sliding in sideways, almost as if one
bird and one bud at a time tested the hospital-

ity of the atmosphere, yet spring is like corn in a popper — first, nothing, and no sign of anything, then one white, full-blown kernel, and suddenly, an explosion of them, beyond counting. Branches are still bare, yet they have lost the dark tones of winter, the attitude of suspension, and there is now some promise to their waving.

("Former Premier Aldo Moro, considered Italy's most influential politician, was kidnapped today by gunmen who killed all five members of his protective escort. A telephone call to ANSA, the Italian news agency, said the kidnappers were from the Red Brigades, Italy's most feared guerrilla group.")

This winding path, about two bushy-tailed foxes wide, and very likely made by them and their colleagues, will be muddy soon, as the sun comes more northerly, but it is firm enough to walk on today. I tread quietly and slowly because spring is, after all, to savor and not to gulp — and my quietness has its reward. At a bend in the path, I come upon a muskrat, sitting up and drying his shiny coat in such weak yellow light as the morning affords.

No matter, it is warmth enough for him; he is well fed and well-coated and his haunches shine in the round. He would have been aware of my presence long before had he not been pleasantly preoccupied with the mating urge. Finally, he discovers me and jumps overboard with a fat plop, more annoyed than alarmed, I think.

("Wind and weather conditions will determine the path of a radiation cloud moving across the Pacific Ocean after a Chinese nuclear test in the atmosphere. The U.S. Energy Department said the first Chinese blast in nearly six months occurred at midnight Tues-

day at the Lop Nor test site in northwestern China.")

Along the shingle of winter-strewn beach, tumbled with windrows of dried weed, gray and black, layered with silvered driftwood worn smooth, and garnished with the litter of life from more seasons by far than I have known, there parade three enormous crows. I sit in a head-high stand of grasses, scrub oak, beach plum, and berry bushes, and watch them come. There is some dignity about them as they eye the water's edge, looking for a shellfish dinner — more dignity when they walk than when hop assuredly, but dignity nonetheless — and they look like clergymen or judges, not of this century, but of the last.

("The Carter administration's top domestic priority should be to halt growing inflation, Federal Reserve Chairman G. William

Miller says. The dollar's poor showing since December will add about 0.75 percent to the inflation rate, he said.")

Within the realm of nature, it does not seem at all unreasonable to discover the centuries overlapping, for surely the irresistible machinery of one spring is much like that of another. Such minor differences as there may have been are obliterated in the pattern of the whole, for natural sequences — having discovered what works well, what is, in fact, practical truth, are willing to stick with it, rather than forever experimenting each year. So far, man has adhered to this principle only with the Volkswagen.

Overhead, there is the lifting cry of geese and there they are, three strungout, wavering "Vs", probably nearly three hundred, high against the pale sky and pumping easily into the northeast.

("A third coal contract agreement, touted by union leaders as greatly improved over the pact buried by a 2-to-1 ballot 11 days ago, is seen in deep trouble because of its health benefits package.")

Now, scientists suggest that the land may be much older than the oceans, rather than vice versa, and that by some massive processes which I do not fully understand, some leisurely, herculean turnings, foldings, uprisings and sinkings, all of this oblate spheroid on which we stand, eat, drink, love, hate, think, dream, struggle, and fear is constantly readjusting, making itself more comfortable, if you will.

I am glad I do not have to watch movement of such proportions; it is unsettling. Here, earth and sea seem stable enough, exchanging pebbles and curls of foam at intervals of about every thirty seconds; this has been going on, I suggest, since my predecessor stood in this place with a stone axe and wondered whether an oyster was edible.

("Contrary to what reporters were told at the State Department last week, the Soviet Union has given little sign that it is prepared to link the end of fighting in the Horn of Africa with reduction of Cuban forces in Ethiopia.")

The dunes, four hundred feet of sand above New England's rock backbone, rise higher at this end of the beach; like French politics (any politics, I guess) they are change that is no change. For, while they are never the same as they were when I was here last, still, they are always here. They are sufficiently fluid in their response to wind and sea to survive, reshaped certainly, but still preserving their fundamental identity and in so doing, are aided immeasurably by the stunted pine, gnarled, hunchbacked, yet determined, that will not let go, no matter what gale or surf.

("The man who allegedly served as a conduit for payments to some of Massachusett's top political figures is under subpoena to testify today before an investigating legislative committee.")

Swinging in a cat-o'-nine-tail clump, a red-wing blackbird gurgles "konk-la-reee," as insistently as the spring presses upon the consciousness.

I will be equally insistent. Having endured the world of man through the winter, I am not about to give up now when the world of nature is promising something much better.

APRIL 2, 1978

In London, once upon a time, there was a drinking place somewhere just north of Soho, near Charlotte Street. It was below the sidewalk and reached by a short flight of stone steps with wrought-iron railings; there was an enormous brass knocker in the shape of a lion's head upon its black door.

It being wartime, the city was largely without illumination after dark and, for the uninitiated, it was easy to miss this place, especially since it had no sign. Most of its customers were American servicemen and they referred to it as "The Lower Bowel," although I suppose it had some other name. Ladies were admitted and there were always a few of them, but never many.

Nothing about the place was distinguished. It held perhaps thirty tables, an obviously ancient bar extended across one end of the room, the ceiling was of beams against white plaster, and the wall-to-wall carpeting was dark enough to conceal drink stains. Most of the lighting came from brass sconces and it was feeble indeed; however no one went there to read, so no one complained and besides, it made all the women look seductive.

I asked a few fellows from time to time why they went there to drink and they all said because it was near. Since I discovered that they came, respectively, from Penarth to the west, Hartlepool to the north, and Lowestoft to the east — all some miles distant — their answer made no sense, but no matter, in wartime, lots of things do not. Roger's Rear Guard made no great sense either but the notion originated in that place and we used to elaborate upon it from evening to evening. For some, it was humorous, for some, it was not.

I never knew Roger's last name. He was an American officer and whenever he was on leave in London, he came to The Lower Bowel and after a couple of drinks, he would go to the piano in the corner and play popular music all evening. His last number of the night was always "Long Ago and Far Away," and since everything was, in fact, precisely that for most present, it sent us home in a nicely suicidal mood.

Roger, one was informed, had a wife at home in the States and a British mistress, whom he loved. Since the war presumably could not last forever, he dreaded the day when he would have to decide whether to leave his wife or his mistress. As time went on, he was more and more sad-eyed, therefore, and although we did not know him much or well, that is why we conceived the idea of a rear guard named for him.

Leftenant Donahue, with whom I was drinking that night, observed, "Look at it this way. There are any number of American servicemen in Roger's situation. When the war's over, they won't want to go home. They'll want to stay with their women over here."

"Why are we going to need an American rear guard here when the war is over?" asked Ensign Hayney.

Donahue said, "Hayney, you are aware that a popular British remark — uttered without the trace of a smile — is that they do not like Americans because they are 'overdressed, overfed, overpaid, oversexed, and over here.' My feeling is that once the war is over, this resentment (in some instances, at least, understandable) will explode and that our departure from these British Isles will be another Dunkirk and we shall need forces to cover our retreat."

"What happens to Roger's Rear Guard after we pull out?" said Hayney.

"Nothing," said Donahue. "Everybody in it would rather stay in Britain than go back to America and they would rather live with Britons than Americans. The British would be thoroughly sympathetic to that sentiment, would think it made great sense, and welcome them all as friends and neighbors."

Still, the concept of Roger's Rear Guard (and I gather he eventually found out about it) was not funny to him. He remained sad-eyed.

The last time I went to The Lower Bowel was in February, 1945. I was on leave from the Seine River area; the Normandy invasion was long behind us, and obviously, the war in Europe was coming to a close. In the drinking place, (most of them possess an illusion of being without time or change) things were largely as they had been. Roger was at the piano; there was a young woman at a table next to him and I concluded it was his British love. As usual, it was too dark in there to tell whether she was pretty. She looked at no one else but him and I thought, "How ironic that the prospect of peace should bring them no peace at all."

One thing had changed. The Germans were firing V-2 rockets at London, on an average of about 60 a week. These things had a one-ton warhead containing 1,600 pounds of high explosive. They were nearly 50 feet long and they traveled in an arc across the Channel, reaching a maximum speed of more than one mile per second and an altitude of 60 to 70 miles. Since the warhead approached the target faster than the speed of sound, there was no warning of the approach of the bomb. Had Hitler been able to get V-2 into production earlier, it undoubtedly would have disrupted

the Allied invasion plans and made London uninhabitable.

Roger was playing "The bells are ringing, for me and my gal," and a few people were singing along, glasses raised, when there was a massive explosion outside — obviously, a V-2. The Lower Bowel shuddered, tables and chairs went over, there was the sound of smashing glass, the wrench of splintering wood and falling plaster, and the lights went out.

There was no panic because everyone there had been through this kind of thing before and because it was obvious that it was not our building that had been struck, even though it was damaged by the blast. And there was no fire, fortunately. One by one, we made our way gingerly through the dark and plaster dust to the street, and to the buildings nearby that had been struck, some of which were burning. Fire apparatus and ambulances wailed, and roared into the area. All of this, too, had happened many times before.

There was what was left of a body in the street, not much more than the headless, naked torso of a young man. The ambulance crew picked it up and put it in a van. It was then that Roger stepped forward and handed something to the medic. Roger said, "You better have this. It was lying next to him. It was his." And the medic said "Thanks. Wouldn't have much to go on without that." And the ambulance drove off.

I know what Roger gave him. He gave the medic his own dog tags, because I saw him take them off a moment before. In so doing, he ended one life and began another, with his British love.

I thought about Roger somewhat when the day finally came to sail from Southampton for New York and the whole business was over. I thought about his sad eyes.

JULY 9, 1978

It was such a day, and such a place, as to make one think inevitably of life, simply because life was everywhere.

Under the grape arbor, precisely where the sun found its way to the tall grass in golden shafts between the leaves, the plump cat drowsed, nose upon paws. In the buckthorn, responding to impulses as fundamental as the axles of the world, a pair of squirrels flowed in their grayness, now like water pouring, now like parentheses, their shoe-button eyes bright. At the foot of the towering pine, a soaked robin stood motionless in the cool comfort of the bird bath and over the fence — in search of a branch, any branch — flopped the young cardinal, still learning the mysteries of flight.

The noises of noon were the only noises, cicada in the clusters of blue flag, great tumbling bees in the honeysuckle, buzzing, and from somewhere far off, a crow's scoldings. In such a moment of fullness, leaf upon leaf, flower upon flower, swaddled in nature's extravagances of sound, color, and smell, it is impossible to ignore the fact of life. The moment itself is alive, sunlight upon the body is life-giving, and all the things and creatures of this warm universe bloom, bustle, browse, and get on with their important businesses.

At such a time, the world seems more enormous than ever, because one is more conscious of its vast going-on and so it is enough for me to try to fathom the largest things by studying the smallest. I lie in the flooding summer heat and watch one small patch of water flowing and think: "Everything, everywhere is symbolized right here. Air, earth, water, creatures, and plants. These are all the ingredients, interacting as they must, in order to keep the whole thing going. And so it has been for centuries beyond counting."

I can measure some of this time past. When I first came to this place, I could stand next to the pine, put my arm straight out and touch the top of it. Now, it towers high above the house; it is a sanctuary in all the seasons for sparrows, grackles and grosbeaks, and meandering skunks dig neat little holes in the carpet of needles beneath it, looking for their dinner. When I could touch the top of the pine, my children where too small to do even that; now, such children as come here are my grandchildren.

It is essentially reassuring to reflect upon the persistence of the natural systems. In a million places, boulders erode; the grindings of this and that catch in crevasses; a seed is blown; the rains come, and something green, driven by the mainspring of life, cracks the damp earth, and emerges in search of light. Something comes by, on wings or feet, and eats it, but it will be back again, and next time, more so.

I watched one small patch of water flowing; there are no fish in it, but because he was doing what I am doing — allowing myself to be mesmerized by a microcosm — I think of D.H. Lawrence. He wrote once: " . . . sitting in a boat on the Zeiler lake/ And watching the fishes in the breathing waters/ Lift and swim and go their way — / . . . A slim young pike, with smart fins/ And a grey-striped suit, a young cub of a pike/ Slouching along away below, half out of sight,/ Like a lout on an obscure pavement . . ./ Aha, there's somebody in the know!"

Well, "in the know," perhaps or perhaps not. I look at the cat, the squirrel, and the robin and think about them, being aware that we have a relationship — we co-exist on this planet and in important ways, what they require to live, I also require. How much they are "in the know," I do not know. They look back at me but I doubt that they are moved to think about me, even if they are capable of doing so. Why on earth should they think about me? It is enough that I do not bother them, so they will let me alone. I have a feeling that if they were given a choice, they would prefer an earth without humans. Occasionally, I feel the same.

Yet I am moved to wonder whether anything other than man consciously aids species other than itself, except where the very young are involved. I am aware that a mother dog will raise an abandoned litter of kittens and so on, and there are parallels among wild creatures, but do the concerns ever go further than this? Man feeds birds, creates wildlife sanctuaries, restocks ponds and streams, attempts to strengthen strains by artificial breeding, and — despite some awful counterproductive practices, including pollution —evidences, at least in the minority, some feeling for what is happening to the flora and fauna.

I am moved to wonder this because I watch one small patch of water flowing and suddenly there is a creature upon its surface. I was going to say that it is a bug of no consequence, a small thing that lost its footing on a leaf above and plopped into the water, but it is both ignorant and insensitive to suggest that it is of no consequence. It is at least of great consequence to itself, even if it cannot even conceive of self, and because I do not even know what kind of bug it is, it could even be of consequence to me because some bugs do, indeed, perform functions that are beneficial to man.

In this small world in which I am engrossed, there now are only two principals, the insect and I, and if I do nothing, there will be only one of us. He is no swimmer; he is in serious trouble, and considering all the relative proportions, he is in the same situation that a non-swimming six-foot man would be in if the latter were roughly three hundred feet from shore.

The insect struggles and I wonder how much he knows about what is happening to him; I wonder if he were my size and I were his, and drowning, whether he would rescue me, ignore me, or eat me.

It is impossible to avoid feeling something like a lower-case omnipotence in this situation. Casual circumstance threw us together in this matter; I hold the power of life and death over this little bug, wiggling frantically, a half-inch of creature.

I pick him up, put him in a sunny corner; he wiggles, stretches, dries out, and ultimately, is off to resume life, largely, one supposes, as if nothing has happened, because I doubt that he will remember.

The interesting thing is that when I picked him up, he bit me but I have to remember that he did not know whether my thumb and forefinger were a robin's beak. Just as I wondered whether he would eat me if our roles were reversed, he had to wonder the same thing about me and after all, that anxiety is part of life, too, isn't it? Besides, what did I expect him to do, curtsy?

JULY 23, 1978

I never pass this particular house — a place of broad chimneys and small panes which has a timeless graciousness without thinking of the most extraordinary dinner party that was held there.

The host, a widower, was in his sixties, and it is characteristic of the whole man that he remained perpetually well groomed, physically fit, and altogether attractive, both to males and females. In his face, mankind was mirrored; strength, joy, tragedy, compassion; in his speech, sparkling with wit, and always with an undercurrent of thoughtfulness, there were words for the world. And his temperament, whatever it may have been before, had been leavened by life and therefore eschewed such aberrations as anger and alarm.

I do not propose to paint him as perfect; had he been, no one would have liked him, I assume — as it was, virtually everybody did. Principally, this was because he was civilized, in the best sense of that word.

He had been a professional person but in these years to which I refer, he was retired and lived very well. His home, filled with books, paintings, and objects collected from a score of countries, was an oasis of culture. There was not one item in that place which was tasteless or ostentatious — or, one supposes, inexpensive. He sailed, fished a little, in perfectionist fashion, interested himself in a greenhouse, and read constantly.

He was a gourmet by inclination. I almost said by heritage, envisioning his taste for pate de foie gras with truffles in canapes as something so much a part of him that it must have been locked into his genes. It was typical of him that I should think that; he gave the impression of having been born well-bred —taste and manners were so much a part of him that one could not imagine any time of his life, however early, when his mother would have had to say to him, "You are holding your fork incorrectly," or whatever.

After his wife died, he was lonely, and out of his interest in good food and wine and his desire to keep in touch with the world, there emerged a very loosely knit group called the Addisonians. What it amounted to was that eight males whom he had known for many years came to his house for dinner, on the third Thursday of each month. He derived great pleasure from selecting the menu, traveling miles to find the best ingredients,

spending up to a couple of days preparing the meal, and keeping the whole business a surprise from them until the moment of serving.

The name of their group — which was his idea — derives from Joseph Addison, who wrote in The Spectator in 1711: "Were I to prescribe a rule for drinking, it should be formed upon a saying quoted by Sir William Temple: the first glass for myself, the second for my friends, the third for good humor, and the fourth for mine enemies." The man of whom I write thought much of Addison's works; this quotation he had had printed on cocktail napkins which were handed in almost ritualistic fashion to his eight guests each month.

On this night in question when they had gathered, it was early October, one of those evenings in which nature chooses to beguile: "There will be no winter this year," she says, and it seems possible because the air is still mild, the wind kind, and the sky powdered with stars.

I owe it to you to tell you about the dinner. It began with escargots bourguignonne, which is to say, snails stuffed into shells, with a mashed clove of garlic in butter poured over, heated in a moderate oven until the butter melts, garnished with parsley and served with chunks of French bread to dip into the sauce. If you have not eaten escargots, pray do not find the notion unthinkable; if you have eaten them, then I assume I do not have to persuade you.

There followed roast squab, each about a pound apiece, and stuffed with a mixture of bread crumbs, parsley, tarragon or basil, paprika, salt, pepper, maybe a little nutmeg, some mushrooms, and melted butter, all preciously baked. The birds were served with stuffed olives and beet pickles, buttered green beans dusted with nutmeg, romaine salad with French dressing, and hot rolls.

The wine was a chilled Graves, a white table wine which comes from Graves district of Bordeaux, in this case, Chateau Haut-Brion. And for dessert, they had strawberries Romanoff — cut the berries into generous pieces, sprinkle with sugar, whip heavy cream until it is stiff, mix it with vanilla ice cream, fold the berries into the mixture, add a jigger of port, and stash in the freezing compartment for an hour before serving. And after that, coffee and brandy.

The affair, as with all of these dinner parties, was a jewel — as if one stepped into the fourth dimension at the front door of his house, leaving behind the scars and bruises of the day, and for these few hours, lived as man ought to live. From the beginning, the nine of them — taking a page from naval officers' wardroom rules — had decided that certain subjects, such as business, politics, sex, and matters likely to produce abrasiveness, would not be discussed at the dinners. The plane of conversation, therefore, tended to be most agreeably ageless and predominantly philosophical. On this particular evening, they had spent nearly an hour discussing what difference it makes where a person lives — that is, what effects upon life style, ambition, longevity, attitude and so on do temperature and climate make?

The phone rang. The host rose from the table, answered it, spoke briefly, and returned. Conversation resumed, during which he finished his brandy, and he then excused himself, saying, "I have to go out to the greenhouse for just a moment."

When he had not returned in a half-hour, they went looking for him. He had shot himself. Time revealed that the phone call was from a law-enforcement officer, that arrest was imminent, because the money that had purchased the host's good life was not his.

Yet I submit that it was typical of him, civilized man that he was, that he should have finished his brandy, completed his conversation, retained his composure, and properly excused himself before putting a bullet through his head.

NOTES AND COMMENTS

An old elevator rattles up to the fifth floor of the *Standard-Times* building in New Bedford. Like other antique newspaper houses, the place carries an air of functional decay, best symbolized by the only sign on a Men's Room door. It reads FIRE ESCAPE. Nearby, overlooking the harbor, is a crow's nest of an office occupied by Everett S. Allen, the great white father of iambic journalism.

He is a striking figure who more resembles a Victorian novelist than a modern journalist. Mutton-chop sideburns decorate his cheeks. His hair, long and whispy in back, is as white as the Great Blizzard of '78. His face has more interesting topographic variety than New Hampshire.

After 41 years at the *Standard-Times*, Allen will soon retire as an editorial writer to begin a book about the history of southern New England. But lovers of creative journalism will welcome the news that Allen's weekly column, "The Present Tense," will continue.

Allen's word-playground is the formal essay, a conventional literary form, but not often found in newspapers. *Essay* derives from a French word meaning "to try," and the etymology applies to Allen's pieces. They are thoughtful attempts to clarify and refine his vision of the world.

That vision is often as hopeful as a brilliant spring day in New England, but is not without its darker side, a brooding realism that calls to mind the poetry of Robert Frost.

Deep, philosophical essays on an op-ed page? Allen has a secret that makes them interesting, readable and relevant. His speculations concern a world of concrete familiarity, a world of tiny animals, burned-down churches, fish chowders, desperate soldiers, mince pies, and genteel old men.

The stories tell much about the man and so does his style. It is clear, graceful, learned, thoughtful and urbane, the style of a man who has spent his life loving the language and being nurtured by it in return. Students of the craft can learn much from Allen's writing:

Description that appeals to the senses — Listen to this sentence: "The noises of noon were the only noises, cicada in the clusters of blue flag, great tumbling bees in the honeysuckle, buzzing, and from somewhere far off, a crow's scoldings."

Concrete images that illustrate abstractions, in this case the passage of time — "I can measure some of this time past. When I first came to this place, I could stand next to the pine, put my arm straight out and touch the top of it. Now, it towers high above the house; it is a sanctuary in all the seasons for sparrows, grackles and grosbeaks, and meandering skunks dig neat little holes in the carpet of needles beneath it, looking for their dinner. When I could touch the top of the pine, my children were too small to do even that; now, such children as come here are my grandchildren."

Complex organization — The structure of the essay on "frozen alertness" follows the wandering process of human thought, seeking unity out of a string of diverse topics: a discussion of a child's eating habits, an economics class, an old man who eats mince pies and stands on his hands. The effective transitions, almost indiscernible, lead us naturally to Allen's conclusion.

Ironic detail — Allen recognizes the effect of Roger's song, "The bells are ringing for me and my gal," minutes before the soldier will change identities for the sake of a lover.

The importance of strong endings — The essays inevitably build to a startling surprise or comic revelation, what James Joyce might have called "an epiphany," a sudden flash of recognition.

The effective use of foreshadowing — After Allen describes his genteel dinner host in terms of the grandest civility, he quickly adds "I do not propose to paint him as perfect." It is a hint of fallibility that will reverberate at the brutal climax of the story.

The power of the short sentence — After a series of long sentences describing the great dinner party, we are hit with the short, ominous sentence "The phone rang." Allen stops us with that sentence, preparing us for the tragic suicide that follows.

In a thoughtful interview, Everett S. Allen discussed his career as a creative journalist, his favorite writers, his sense of style and his respect for his readers.

Interview with Roy Clark and Everett Allen

CLARK: How would you describe your column "The Present Tense?"

ALLEN: The title of the column was "The Present Tense," but I thought of that as meaning we are, we remember, we hope. So that it covers all the tenses there are. It also covers all the subjects there are. I like the essay. I try to suggest something of larger proportions by writing about something of smaller proportions.

Isn't it unusual to be writing formal essays for a newspaper?

We are not in the Fourth Estate well thought of. Part of the reason is that we have grown away from people. That is why I like the idea of the personal essay as a means of getting to people, of reaching out to them. I purposely, for example, do not nail the locale down. I don't use the specific names of places. One time I wrote the story of a church that burned in a small town. I received a number of calls from people who knew exactly where the church was and where the community was. And they all had a different church, a different community. But they related to the story.

Aren't these essays too sophisticated for your readers?

A woman called me one Monday in what I thought was a rather touching fashion and said that she could not use the words that I had used in the particular piece, but she understood their meaning. This is the point. People have two vocabularies. One they use, the other they understand. I am mindful of that. I never write down to these people. If there is a proper word, one that is a really good word, that's the word I use. I am also a great believer in detail with the idea that you hold the moment or the incident aloft so that people can look at it. And you hold it there long enough, and you turn it enough so they can see all sides of it, and maybe you even peel it the way you would the layers of an onion until they realize what the thing is.

Do you think there should be more places in newspapers for the kind of writing you do?

I suppose there is less place for this than I wish. On the other hand, maybe simply because it's uphill, it's not impossible. I think we have become obsessed with politics and government. They are so much of our lives. So many of our people who write columns are concerned with matters of government. My column is something else. To my mind, we should have better communication between ourselves and the readers. One thing that bothers readers is the feeling that they can't reach us or know us. I'm not sure they think that people who write for newspapers are the same as other people. I have the feeling that they think we are arrogant and that they suspect the everyday things of life rarely happen to us. I wrote a piece one time about falling down a manhole. It was one of the most popular things I ever did. I think they were glad to know that anyone who worked for a newspaper fell down a manhole. It shows a certain fallibility that they found human, and the results I think were rather amusing — in retrospect.

Some of your stories read like fiction, they have the feel of short stories. Are they factual?

Yes. When I started this column, I explained to my editors that these would be based on incidents in real life. The people span many years as do the events. I sometimes put them together to suit my convenience. I may put together two or three events. But all the events happened.

What literary influences can be drawn to your work?

There are some people whom I love and rather live with in my thinking. The first two who come to mind are Robert Frost and Edna St. Vincent Millay. I have thought a great deal of them. Carl Sandburg is another one. It's odd, in a way, that I should think of poets. As a student I had some loose contact with Frost at Middlebury College. I interviewed Carl Sandburg. But Millay? I don't know. I've loved her from a distance all these years. And Thoreau. I'm a great admirer of E.B. White. I am in love with the language. And therefore I would not only love E.B.

White, but Dr. Strunk as well. And humor. I love White's humor. Humor is an essential lubricant.

You quote literary figures — like Lawrence and Addison — often in your columns. Aren't you afraid of losing your readers?

I had a phone call from a woman. My column runs on Sunday. She called one Monday. She said "I do not have any education and I'm not going to tell you who I am. I cannot read your column on Sunday because my husband would laugh at me. So I save it and read it on Monday. I read it this morning and I just wanted to tell you how much I like it." O.K. so they lose a word here and there. Maybe they don't. But the truth is the truth. I speak a language that I think most people can understand.

I see a consistent philosophical outlook in your work that has both a dark and a hopeful side.

I've done a lot of pieces about the war, and I suppose one underlying theme, no matter which incident I use, is the ability of the human creature to endure through great trials, on the one hand, and the terrible poignancies that were associated with war which had nothing to do with being shot at. Our community, for example, has many ethnic strains. I once called this place a little united nations. Their roots are very deep so I could not delude them. But I like to remind them periodically through these little incidents that just when you have given up on man, he is for no particularly logical reason courageous enough to command admiration, selfless enough to be incredible, triumphant in failure, so that you come away with a sense of his ability to endure. There is a certain cyclical quality about what I feel. I do go into sloughs of depression. But the public is my psychiatrist, and the writing is therapeutic. If I get depressed, I level with these people. I always feel better once I've written myself through the thing. Once when I was depressed, I found myself writing a column about fish chowder. I philosophized about the people over the centuries who had caught fish and raised potatoes and talked about the geometry of an onion, for example, and of the durability of the codfish, even in an age of pollution and overfishing. It made me feel better. The people who read what I write know a great deal about me. And you're right, there's a dark side and a light side.

How do you go about writing a column?

I never rewrite. I write very rapidly. I don't write from notes. I just sit down and write it. The average column takes me from 8 to about 10 o'clock on Sunday morning. I write it a week in advance of publication. And I write at home in a studio that I built with my own hands. There are birds and cats and dogs outside and it seems more in keeping with the realities of life than does a newspaper office.

You write a lot about nature.

I grew up on Martha's Vineyard in the 1920s. If you grew up there it was impossible not to be close to the changing seasons. It's the first thing you're locked into because you know when the herring are going to run and you know when the eels are coming in, or when you can catch haik or mackerel. You are related to the clock of the universe. I did a story about two cardinals who lived in our backyard. A hurricane came and blew the female bird away. The male bird grieved for eight or nine days, and I was upset all week long. Anyway, on the tenth day they were reunited. I said in conclusion that I didn't know if I could stand another hurricane, even though the cardinals probably could. I had a tremendous reaction from people who I dare say had never even seen a cardinal. But they were touched by the plight of these birds whose basic instincts were monogamous. If you will, they loved each other.

Let's talk about writing style. What are the things you value most in your writing?

I am a great believer in description. I try to make the reader feel that he can see and taste and smell and touch and hear whatever the incident is. I've just listed the five senses. I am subtly conscious of appealing to each one of them in turn. I am conscious of word choice, especially conscious of how a sentence begins. I am aware of sentence length. I sometimes have quite long sentences. It doesn't bother me. But I am conscious of the effectiveness among long sentences of one that has only two words. You really snap them up short.

You obviously work on the endings of your stories. They all seem to end with a dramatic climax or a humorous insight.

It's deliberate.

Let's say a student of journalism picks up this book and reads your columns. What would you like that student to learn about writing from your work?

First of all grammar. I have examined several dozen job applications from people with college degrees and obviously nobody has taught them grammar. One thing they might learn is the importance of *le mot juste* — what is the word that we need. I like to think of the right word quickly, without having to fiddle around with it. Speed is a skill that they ought to work at. They should try to have a feeling for

— maybe beauty is too highflown a word — a feeling for the effective and careful structure of the sentence. I would hope they would think carefully about their first paragraph. It is as important as the first chapter of a book. Either you grab the reader or you don't. I hope they would think about the rhythm of the piece so that it doesn't hitch and haul or turn back on itself, so that in a subtle and inconspicuous way it flows. Above all, I would hope that they would sense in these articles a thoughtful bridge between the academic world and the world of journalism. The newspaper, in a sense, is the book of the masses. So I hope they wouldn't think that if they're going to work for a newspaper, they wouldn't be able to write anymore.

Is it possible for American newspapers to give greater value to creative writing?

I hope that American newspapers recognize the need to nurture good writing in young people coming along. I think in every newsroom there could be one person who is a *writer*, and one person who is an *editor*, and who would be professionally married. So when this editor sees a good story come along, he would be able to turn his good writer loose on it. I realize the limitations of time and space, but even if it were no longer than half a column, turn out a small gem, once a week, twice a week, that people read even if they're not interested in the subject. Yet they read it because of the manner in which it's put together. Because it's put together with love, with care. This is great.

ALLEN'S REMARKS

On receiving the American Society of Newspaper Editors' award at the banquet of the New York convention, Everett S. Allen said:

I am profoundly grateful for all the obvious reasons, yet grateful beyond these for one reason which may not be at all obvious.

When I was about to graduate from college, one of my English professors, who apparently thought well of me, called me to his office. He said, "I believe that you have some ability to write and I am therefore most depressed to learn that you have decided to go into journalism."

At the moment, I was in no position to reply, but I resented the remark. In part, that may have been why I made such an effort, from the very beginning, to inject the best writing of which I was capable into such news stories as were assigned to me.

I believe that I am the only newspaper reporter who deliberately and successfully inserted in a general-alarm fire story a perfect iambic line. I was so titillated at being able to do it — and in getting it past the copydesk, and you know how copydesks are about perfect iambic lines — that even though it was something like 38 years ago, I remember it perfectly.

The line was, "Ten pumpers roared throughout the night in Sawyer Street." Now, if 13 pumpers had shown up at the fire, or if the fire had been, let us say, in Brock Avenue, I would have had to either (a) change the meter of the line, or (b) respectfully decline to cover the fire.

Happily, I did not have to make either choice. And since that time, I have persisted in attempting to introduce creative writing into the news columns whenever possible and, in these latter years, that has meant encouraging the young to do likewise.

I am most pleased that my peers, the prestigious leadership of ASNE, have, through the creation of these awards, moved to provide fresh and important incentive to those on American newspaper staffs who can and wish to write creatively.

Cover, author portraits and design by Diane Tonelli

Illustrations on pages 11, 21, 31, 52, 61, 71, 92, 101, 110, 129, 135, 142 and 156 by Joe Tonelli